Bill Heritage

*Ponds and
Water Gardens*

BLANDFORD PRESS
Poole   New York   Sydney

First published in the U.K. 1981 by Blandford Press,
Link House, West Street,
Poole, Dorset BH15 1LL

Copyright © 1981 and 1986 Blandford Press Ltd.

Reprinted 1982
Reprinted 1983
Reprinted 1984
Reprinted 1985 (twice)
Revised edition 1986

British Library Cataloguing in Publication Data

Heritage, Bill
 Ponds and water gardens.—2nd ed.
 1. Water gardens
 I. Title
 635.9'674   SB423

ISBN 0-7137-1861-7 Paperback
    0-7137-1882-X Hardback

Phototypeset in Monophoto Apollo by
Asco Trade Typesetting Ltd., Hong Kong

Printed in Hong Kong by South China Printing Co.

Contents

Acknowledgements

A number of people have made valued contributions to the completion of this book and I would like to take this opportunity to express my gratitude first and foremost to Irene, wife, typist and helpmeet; to my friend and colleague Michael D. Everett, Managing Director of Wildwoods Water Gardens, Enfield, Middlesex, for generously sharing his expertise in all to do with pumps; to Norman and Jonathan Bennett who gave so much time and effort to the photographic sessions at Bennetts Water Lily and Fish Farm, Chickerell, Weymouth, Dorset, which produced most of the water lily portraits, and to Robin Fletcher, who took the best of them; to Mr and Mrs Martin Acland, Mr and Mrs Michael Harris, Mr and Mrs Winston Ramsey, and Nuffield College, Oxford, for permission to photograph their splendid gardens; to David Everett, Joe Payne, Peter Robinson and Jim Saunders who also helped with material and facilities for photography; to W.H.L. Mann, R.J.G. Reeve, Graham Scarlett and Ted Uber for stimulating ideas and helpful information and suggestions; to Frances Perry, upon whose original researches and classic book *Water Gardening* all subsequent writers have leaned so heavily; and to Gladys Winifred Thorburn.

The publishers gratefully acknowledge the following for permission to reproduce illustrations. Colour: the author (**2, 3, 4, 5, 8, 9, 10, 11, 12, 13, 15, 16, 18, 19, 23, 24, 26, 27, 28, 29, 30, 32, 34, 35, 38, 39, 40, 41, 42, 43, 45, 46, 48, 49, 50, 51, 52, 53, 54, 55, 56, 57, 58, 59, 60, 61, 62, 63, 64**); Robin Fletcher (**1, 6, 7, 14, 17, 20, 21, 22, 25, 31, 33, 36, 37, 44, 47**). Black and white: Laurence E. Perkins (pp. 12, 18, 34, 120, 123 lower, 127, 151); Heather Angel, Biofotos (pp. 121, 123 upper).

Preface

To anyone who has ever had a garden pool no explanation of its varied delights is necessary. The gleam of water, the tranquil beauty of lily blooms sailing among cloud reflections, the swirl of rising fish, the chuckle of a cascade, and the heady scent of water hawthorn are, for those who have known them, pleasures without which no garden can be regarded as complete.

Nevertheless, unlikely as it will seem to these initiates, there are still gardeners who need to be persuaded; who require assurance that the effort involved in creating a water garden will be adequately rewarded; that there are sound practical reasons for going to the trouble of adding water to the garden scene. The following pages will indicate, I hope, that it is much less trouble than many people imagine and that the dividends in interest and enjoyment for the whole family are enormous.

Some of them are obvious enough. The gardener in the family will discover how very easily water lilies can be persuaded to produce magnificent flowers. Those members of the family who normally take no notice of the garden at all will be found to take a lively interest in the occupants of the pond and to share the general satisfaction in the successful rearing of 'home-grown' fish. Children will find tadpoles and newts and all the other busy members of the pool community endlessly fascinating.

Among many virtues, the water garden has two qualities that are outstanding. More than any other garden feature it commands attention. It creates the focal point that so many gardens lack. Its magnetic attraction draws the footsteps and gives purpose to aimless paths. It seems somehow to gather the rest of the garden comfortably around it, giving both a focus and a unity to the whole.

Then there is the gift of relaxation. While other parts of the garden wear the reproachful look that nags of work needing doing, the water garden requires not that we hurry but that we pause. It reminds us that there should be time to stand and stare, or, preferably, to sit and stare; or better still, to have tea by the pool and, between bites, to flick titbits to the fish cruising underneath the lily pads.   BH 1980

5

1
Introduction

Garden ponds are made for a variety of reasons. Depending on the primary interest of the maker, the end product can range from an elaborate system of torrential waterfalls, streams and cascades to the vast outdoor fish tank, with a sophisticated filtration system and the proportions of a small swimming pool, that a Koi fancier constructs for his charges. In neither of these examples is there much place – or much hope of survival – for the beautiful aquatic plants which many gardeners see as the main reason for having a pond.

The fact is that water gardening is not a single subject but a blend of several; a mixture in which ingredients can be varied, emphasised or even omitted altogether according to the particular interests of the owner. Although most facets of the subject will, I hope, get fair treatment in the following pages, it seems only right to declare my own preference for a garden pond that is a bit of everything, a water garden in which 'garden' is the operative word, where plants, though only part of a scheme that includes fish and moving water and the natural community of aquatic creatures, have pride of place.

For me a water garden is, first and foremost, an area devoted to the cultivation of interesting and ornamental plants whose natural habitat is in or near water. It will invariably include a body of water, whether a lake, a pond or merely a tub, to accommodate purely aquatic plants. It may also embrace an area of soil not covered with water, but permanently moist, which is generally referred to as a bog garden. This is an optional extra with virtues and drawbacks that will be discussed later. The water garden may include moving water arrangements to create fountains or waterfalls provided they are limited to a scale which will not be detrimental to the plants. Moving water is also an optional extra. It has benefits and disadvantages. It makes delightful music but does not perform some of the miracles claimed for it. Certainly it is not essential and a completely static pool can be completely successful.

Fish should always be present, for more than simply practical and ornamental reasons. It is very agreeable to have them rush towards you, in response to a couple of taps on the pool surround, in the

Visibility is a prime virtue in pond fish and from this point of view a plain red goldfish is hard to beat.

confident expectation of being fed, and immensely satisfying, regardless of whether they measure up to show standards, to have a pond full of lively, healthy, friendly fish.

At this point it should be made clear that in the general-purpose plant-orientated water garden that this book is about there is no place for the Koi carp. It is a magnificent fish, given the right treatment, but in ponds depending on natural balance it is frequently a failure. If it survives, few plants will survive with it. To thrive, it needs a large area of deep water and a substantial filtration system. It is a fish apart, with specialised needs (and a specialist literature), and subsequent considerations of pond size, depth and so on do not embrace the highly individual needs of the Koi carp.

Flourishing plants and thriving fish are the aim and the reward of a well managed pond. They will be the star performers and everything possible must be done to encourage them. There are no two ways about it: the first duty of the would-be water gardener is not to indulge his own whims and fancies of pond design until he is satisfied that they will please the occupants of the pond as much as they will please him. His first concern must always be to provide the best possible conditions for plants and fish. This will be the test of every proposal concerning the size, the shape, the depth and the position for the pond, and the arrangement of any moving water features.

Water lilies are lovers of light. The more sunshine they get the better they will flower. Some marginal plants will tolerate dappled shade but most need, and all will enjoy, the sunniest site possible.

Very few ornamental aquatic plants have any tolerance of currents. Water lilies in particular like static water that can warm up quickly. Any water movement discourages them and flowing streams or spring-fed pools suit them least of all.

Fish need unpolluted well-oxygenated water that does not become overloaded with carbon dioxide. They will tolerate water movement but do not demand it. Splashing water is what they enjoy; the mere movement of cross-pool currents does nothing for them at all.

Algae are simple forms of plant life. Wherever there is light and water, algae in one form or another will occur. The pea-soup green discoloration of pond water consists of vast numbers of single-celled algae. The choking masses of blanketweed are the strands of filamentous algae. Algae are plants and they thrive on sunlight.

These are the basic facts of life with which the water gardener has to contend. It might seem that they cannot all be compatible with the aim of creating a water garden where fish can enjoy the benefits of water movement without the plants being inhibited; where there is a luxuriant growth of flowering plants without an abundance of blanketweed; and where water lilies will bloom bounteously and the colourful movement of fish still be seen through gin-clear water.

Is this impossible? By no means. Never forgetting that the needs of plants and fish take precedence over all else, and mindful of the facts of life already outlined, let us apply logic, ingenuity and a touch of compromise to the practical details of pond position, size, shape and stocking, and see what emerges.

2
Design and Construction

Position

The best position for a pond is the one that gets the most sunshine. Any notion that a water garden would be just the thing to brighten up a dark corner can be dismissed out of hand. The 'ferned grot' beloved of Victorians, with its trickle of water in a gloomy recess overhung with ferns, is not the sort of water garden that this book is about. It is about a place to sit in the sun and enjoy the blooms of water lilies and water iris and marsh marigolds. A really bounteous display will be provided only in return for a place in the sun. Sunshine for five hours a day is what is needed; if there can be more, so much the better. Water lilies, whose natural lake habitats are open to all the light there is, cannot have too much sunshine.

Nevertheless, as has already been said, sunshine is what algae thrive on too. It seems that we are faced with a dilemma almost before we have started. The obvious solution, to many gardeners, is to put the pond in the shade of trees, hoping thus to avoid the nuisance of green water and blanketweed, and keeping their fingers crossed as far as the effect on flowering is concerned. In doing so they create problems for the future that can never be adequately resolved. They lose more than the optimum flowering performance of their lilies. Trees, in addition to casting shade, annually shed large quantities of leaves, pollen, petals, twigs, bud scales, and seeds, berries, or fruit. This detritus, rotting in the pond, pollutes the water with the noisome by-products of decay, with at least harmful, and possibly fatal, results for the fish. Some trees are particularly damaging. The leaves of willows and poplars contain aspirin, and the leaves, flowers and seeds of laburnum are actively poisonous; but rotting leaves of *any* kind, in large quantities, produce the same dire consequences.

So keep the pond as far away from trees and overhanging bushes as possible. Put it in the most open sunny position you can find. What happens? Single-celled algae, quickest to take advantage of the conditions, colour the water green while lilies are still getting settled in. With their roots well established the lilies begin to unroll leaves on the surface. Grateful for the warm water and the sunshine, the lilies respond by spreading broad pads across the surface to soak up the sunlight. In using it themselves, of course, they also deny it to the algae. As more of the surface is covered by leaves, less and less light gets past the surface and the algae dwindle. If the surface was totally covered no light would enter the water at all and no algae in any form would be able to survive; but that would be bad for various other life forms too, and total coverage is not intended. Something between a half and two-thirds of the surface covered with leaves will do nicely, and this is a figure to bear in mind when it comes to deciding how many lilies and other surface-covering plants the pond will need. If it is objected that two-thirds of the surface covered with foliage reduces the chances of seeing the fish, the answer must be that they will be visible much more frequently if the uncovered third is clear water than if 90 per cent of the surface is open to the sun and the water is as thick as pea soup. The fish, in any case, are much less likely to spend their time skulking on the bottom if there is enough surface cover to give them a feeling of security from predators.

A sunny, open position, then, well clear of trees, is the first essential. Other considerations affecting the choice of pond site are visibility, accessibility and services. It is pleasant to be able to catch the glint of water from the house without even stirring outdoors, but it should, perhaps, not be so directly under a window that the eye cannot be averted from the pond's inevitably lifeless and chilling aspect in the winter. During the summer months at least the pond will draw the footsteps like a magnet; therefore it will save extra work if, all other needs being satisfied, it can be sited near an existing path. A reasonable area of paving on at least one side of the pond is essential. If the pond is of any size it should have a path on three sides at least so that all its details can be comfortably examined. They should be good, wide, strolling two-abreast paths. Water will be required for initial filling and occasional topping up, so the pond should not be beyond the convenient reach of the hose. Since pumps and lights and pond heaters require electricity, an undercover socket outlet not too far away will prove a great convenience.

In the unlikely event that the site which fulfils all these requirements turns out to be the one spot in the garden where all the surface drainage, and an impervious soil layer beneath, create a permanently waterlogged hollow, just strike it off the list and go for the next best choice. It might seem the obvious place for a pond but in fact it is not. It will never be sufficiently drought-proof to make a natural pond and it is the worst place possible in which to make an artificial one, because of the difficulties of carrying out any form of construction in an excavation partly filled with water. In such a situation, it is possible for a liner to float to the surface because of the pressure of water beneath it.

Pond Size

It is very understandable that someone contemplating pond construction for the first time should approach an unfamiliar subject with some caution. Just in case it does not turn out well, he resolves not to be carried away. He decides to start with something small and, if that works out well, attempt bigger things later. This is a very sensible approach if it is applied to the over-all water garden project: for example, make the pond first and postpone the pump and waterfall system until later; then think about some lighting, perhaps, later still. If these things are allowed for in the original concept there is certainly no rush to complete the whole scheme all at one go and it may well make sense to spread the cost over several seasons of steady progress.

If this approach is applied to the pond itself, however, if it involves starting with a little pond and seeing what happens, then disappointment is almost bound to follow. Where ponds are concerned small is not beautiful (not very often anyway). The smaller the pond the more precarious is the balance between success and failure; the more likely it is to be plagued with problems; and the more likely it is to remain permanently and offensively green. From many contacts with pond-owners over many years it is very clear that satisfaction is in direct proportion to pond size. Big is beautiful, in this context at least. Bigger means less temperature fluctuation and a greater stability of environment that will benefit all the pond's occupants. Bigger means a more easily attained, more certain, self-sustaining ecological balance – but bigger than what? The critical size seems to be something in the region of 50 square feet of surface area (see Metric Conversion Table for equivalents). Make it bigger by all means, make it, indeed, as big as space and pocket will allow, but do not make it much less, if you can possibly help it, than 50 square feet. If this seems a lot, think of it in terms of a square with 7-foot sides, or a rectangle 10 by 5 feet, or a circle 8 feet across. There are very few gardens in which that sort of space cannot be found, and many in which it would seem ridiculously small in proportion to the whole. It can be illuminating to mark it out on the ground with a length of hose or clothes line. If it looks miniscule, modify the dimensions until the scale looks right. At the same time, experiment with shape.

Pond Shape

It is usually a good idea, with any sort of garden planning, to get something down on paper. In designing a garden pond the sketching of alternative shapes may certainly help to clarify ideas but can also prove to be a trap for the unwary. To the novice simple squares, circles or ovals seem to lack inspiration and he is tempted into elaborations. Edges are scalloped, arms are developed, a waist is pinched in perhaps (with visions of a rustic bridge, going nowhere) and a sort of canal may even be led round the garden and back to the pond. All this is done to make it a more 'interesting' shape. Interesting it may be on paper, but the trap into which the designer falls is forgetting that he will never see it from this aerial plan view. He will not even spend much time looking at it from an upstairs window. His elaborate scheme will be viewed at a low angle across the garden, and it will look very different from the plan. Suppose that there is a pond surround of 2-inch thick paving, and suppose that the water surface is an inch or two below the level of the underside of the paving. Viewed even from 10 yards away the narrow arms and serpentine squiggles will virtually disappear and scarcely a gleam of water will be visible. Visitors hurrying to view the pond may well be in some danger of falling in before they realise that they have reached it.

The most useful diagrams are those drawn on the ground with that length of clothes line. They will give the best impression of how the pond will appear seen across the garden. It will be found that the simple shape is, after all, the best. It will, of course, need to conform to the style of its surroundings. If the chosen site is on a patio, or in a rectangle of lawn framed by straight paths and borders, then a formal circle or rectangle will suit it and an irregular 'natural' shape will not. If the pond is to adjoin a rockery in association with curving lawns and borders then clearly a rectangle will be unsuitable; either an irregular shape or a circle would be needed. The circle, or something close to it, is in fact the best shape for most situations, because whichever way you look at it you will look across its full width. That, of course, should be the aim: the widest possible stretch of water to gather light and gleam invitingly from afar, to catch the spray of a fountain and have room for the uncramped spread of water lilies too. It is best to forget all about canals and 'interesting' shapes and such 'whimsies' as bridges and islands. Keep the shape open and simple and make sure that whatever space is allocated to the water garden is filled with as much water as possible.

13

The mottled colouring of Shubunkins, seen to great advantage in an aquarium, is less conspicuous (even producing a camouflage effect) in the very different lighting and background conditions of a garden pond.

Pond Depth

The depth of the pond is determined by several factors. The needs of plants and fish are, as always, of paramount importance. Then there is the possible effect of depth (and consequently volume) on the question of pond balance and the risk of algae problems. Not least is the need to avoid wasting effort in digging any deeper than is absolutely necessary. Happily, it is possible to avoid a great deal of unneccessary labour simply by disposing of two long cherished water garden myths.

One is the notion that in order to grow the hardy lilies with the largest flowers it is necessary to plant them in 3 or 4 feet of water. The truth is that while some of the strongest growers will just about tolerate that much if they are pushed, they certainly do not need it. They have a wide depth tolerance and will grow perfectly well with 15 inches of water over them – and flower better into the bargain. A glance at the selection guide (pp. 38–9) will show that a planting depth of 15 inches comes within the depth tolerance limits of more than 80

14

per cent of the varieties listed. Add 8 or 9 inches for soil depth and it is clear that even for the largest hardy lilies a maximum pond depth of 24 inches is enough. The chart also shows that a pond depth of 15 inches, allowing 9 inches of water over 6 inches of soil, would cater for all the hardy lilies except the vigorous Group VI and Group VII varieties.

The second myth concerns fish, for whose safety in winter a section 4 or 5 feet deep was once believed to be necessary. It is difficult to understand the logic of this. The possibility of ice forming to a greater depth than 8 or 9 inches is remote in most temperate zones such as Britain even in very severe winters. The real danger to fish comes from the build up of toxic gases from decaying organic matter in the pond which cannot escape because the surface is sealed by a layer of ice. The thickness of the ice is immaterial; it is its persistence for a few weeks (or even one if the pond is clogged with dead leaves) that does the damage. The fish die from suffocation, not from cold, and they die, in this situation, whether the pond is 2 feet or 5 feet deep. Going deeper, where the water holds less dissolved oxygen, is no help. The answer to this problem is to keep a hole open in the ice, not to dig a deeper hole.

Any pond depth between 15 and 24 inches will, it seems, meet the needs of fish and offer a wide choice of lilies. So is there, in fact, any reason to go beyond 15 inches? There is, and this has to do with volume. If the water is 24 inches deep, every square foot of water surface area will have 2 cubic feet of water beneath it, and 2 cubic feet equals $12\frac{1}{2}$ (Imperial) gallons. If the water depth is 15 inches, each square foot of the surface will have less than 8 gallons of water beneath it. This ratio of gallonage to surface area becomes significant when the effect of sunlight falling on the open surface is considered. The shallower the pond the fewer gallons will there be to absorb the sun's effects; the degree of heating and light penetration will be greater and so, in consequence, will the occurrence and persistence of algae.

The over-all volume/surface area ratio of a pond will be influenced by the profile, or sectional shape. We have seen that a pond with vertical sides and a uniform depth of 15 inches will contain barely 8 gallons per square foot of surface area. If that pond was saucer-shaped and 15 inches deep only at one point, then the ratio would be a mere 4 gallons per square foot. This is simply licensing algae to run riot and explains why a saucer shape (which has, into the bargain, no horizontal planting surfaces) is the worst possible shape for a pond.

The maximum ratio of volume to surface area would be achieved if the pond had vertical sides and a uniform depth. Vertical sides are not feasible for constructional reasons, but at least they can be steeply sloped, at about 20 degrees to the vertical.

The pond profile must also cater for a group of plants whose needs have not yet been considered. They are the marginals, such as irises and bulrushes, which grow with their roots covered by only a few inches of water. They are provided for in concrete ponds by built-in troughs or corner pockets and in either concrete or liner ponds by a shelf 10 to 12 inches wide and 8 or 9 inches below water level. The shelf need not run all round. It can be continuous or interrupted but need add up to no more than about a third of the total perimeter. This marginal shelf and the main floor of the pool are the only planting levels needed. Assuming that container planting will be used, any fine adjustments in depth to suit individual plants can be made easily enough by propping containers on tiles or bricks. There is absolutely no need for the pond profile to incorporate a staircase of different levels. The pond profile, indeed, is very much simpler than has sometimes been represented. Its salient features can be summarised as follows.

Sides sloped at 20 degrees to the vertical (which amounts to 1 inch in for every 3 inches down).
Marginal shelf (continuous or interrupted, as desired) 10 to 12 inches wide and 8 or 9 inches below water level.
Maximum depth (applying to the whole pond apart from marginal shelves) never less than 15 inches, and preferably 18 inches, for ponds less than 40 square feet in surface area. From 40 to 100 square feet a depth of 18 inches is permissible but 24 inches is strongly recommended: even more insistently beyond 100 square feet. Beyond 300 square feet one might go to $2\frac{1}{2}$ or 3 feet but there is no case for anything deeper.

Volume/surface area ratios can only be estimated approximately but, assuming a pool of 100 square feet surface area and estimating for the effect of shelves, containers and sloping sides, they should be roughly as follows.

> For 15 in maximum depth: $6\frac{1}{2}$ gallons/sq ft.
> For 18 in max. depth: 8 gals/sq ft.
> For 24 in max. depth: 11 gals/sq ft.
> For 30 in max. depth: 14 gals/sq ft.
> For 36 in max. depth: $16\frac{1}{2}$ gals/sq ft.

Experience suggests that anything over 10 gallons per sq ft is excellent; 8 to 10 is adequate; 5 to 7 invites problems; and anything under 5 is likely to be disastrous.

A picture now emerges of the ideal pool: a pool that will make a satisfactory home for fish and for a wide choice of water lilies and other plants; a pool whose excellent volume/surface area ratio will encourage environmental stability and minimise problems; a pool that will require no more exertion by its maker than is absolutely necessary. It will have a sunny position and a simple open shape. It will be at least 50 square feet in surface area, and as much more as its owner can find the space and the courage for. It will have steep sides, a marginal shelf, and a main floor depth of 24 inches.

Alternative Construction Methods
Before the picture can be translated into reality a decision has to be made about the materials to be employed. Not so very long ago there was no choice: it had to be concrete. Now, to the great relief of those who found concrete not only a back-breaking and intractable material but one that all too often failed to hold water, there are alternatives available that are more reliable and require much less effort. They are not all perfect, and their pros and cons will be examined in due course.

Two points of constructional detail must first be made which apply to all ponds, whatever they are made of. The first and most vital is the question of level. Nothing looks worse than a pond with water lapping over the rim at one end and several inches below it at the other, but a surprising number of pond-makers do not discover this until it is too late to do anything about it, because it never occurred to them to use a spirit level. However level the ground may appear it is essential to use a length of straight timber and a spirit level to make sure that the rim of the finished pool, whether it be concrete or glassfibre or a liner, is level from end to end and side to side. Secondly, when the paving is laid around the edge, how is it to relate to adjoining surfaces? If, for example, the paving is required to be flush with adjacent turf, then a 2-inch layer must be excavated over the area to be occupied by pond plus paving before beginning to excavate the pond profile.

The matter of pond drains and overflows can soon be dispensed with. They are not necessary. An overflow is needed only if there is a continuous supply of water flowing into the pond, and such an arrangement is highly undesirable. A plughole in the bottom, apart from creating structural weaknesses, simply results in the erosion of soil beneath the pond base, the creation of a cavity, and eventual disaster.

Concrete
A concrete pond has a satisfying texture that cannot be equalled by other materials. It has great strength, but that strength can be destroyed by its inflexibility. Under the stresses imposed by an expanding sheet of thick ice, or by the settlement or shrinkage of the subsoil, it cannot bend and is bound to crack. A cracked concrete pond is worse than no pond at all, since there is no certain way of repairing it. The secrets of success in making a concrete pond are careful preparation beforehand, speed once the job is started, and meticulous attention to every detail along the way. There can be no skimping and there are no short cuts.

The simplest pond shape to make with concrete would be a saucer, but this has already been ruled out. The need for steep sides demands the use of shuttering to prevent the sidewall concrete from slumping to the base before it is set. Shuttering consists of wood or chipboard cross-braced with lengths of timber to hold it firmly in the required shape. Relatively easy for a rectangular pool, it becomes much more difficult if the shape is informal. Hardboard rather than chipboard can be used to achieve the desired curves.

The hard labour called for in concrete construction begins with digging the hole 5 inches larger all round than the proposed pond size, to allow for the thickness of concrete and rendering, with an additional 5 inches below the base to accommodate the hardcore foundation which will (it is hoped) minimise the effect of any subsequent subsoil shrinkage.

When the excavation is done the hardcore mixture of coarse gravel, stones and rubble must be rammed very firmly into place. The same materials can with advantage be tamped into the sides to make a firm backing for the concrete. Before the next stage – the mixing and laying of the concrete – everything necessary must be to hand so that, once started, the job will be completed in the shortest possible time. The shuttering and frame must be ready, tools must be assembled, and there must be no risk of running out of the raw materials. These, though mixed by volume, will generally be bought by weight. For every 10 square feet of superficial area (bottom, sides and shelves) allow $\frac{1}{2}$ cwt of cement, 1 cwt of sharp sand, 2 cwt of coarse aggregate (1 inch down) and $1\frac{1}{4}$ lb of waterproofing powder.

First mix the appropriate amount of waterproofing powder into the cement. Then, measuring by volume (so many buckets of each) mix 3 parts of aggregate for every 2 parts of sharp sand and 1 of cement. It is vital that they be very thoroughly mixed *dry* before adding water, still mixing, to achieve a 'stiff' paste that is firm enough to be cut into slices. Spread the mixture on the pool floor about 2 inches thick, add reinforcing steel mesh or chicken wire, then spread and level another 2 inches of the mixture on top, making sure no wire protrudes. This is a good point at which to break for rest and refreshment, because it will be thirty minutes to an hour before the base is firm enough to install the shuttering frame, if it can be done without walking on the base. Now form the walls by filling the space between the shuttering and the side of the excavation, and be sure that as one mix is used up another is being prepared, to avoid hold-ups.

By having everything ready for an early morning start the average-sized garden pond can usually be completed in one arduous day. It will take longer with a large design where shuttering cannot be installed without walking on the base because of the need to wait a day or two for the base to be firm enough. It is important not to delay longer than absolutely necessary, and to roughen up the edges of the base, to achieve a satisfactory join between base and walls. Once the basic shell is complete, including the formation of any desired shelf or marginal trough, the rendering coat should be added as soon as the concrete is firm enough to work. This may be a matter of days, depending on the weather, and if it is hot wet sacks should be laid on the concrete to prevent too rapid drying. The rendering consists of 1 part of cement (with waterproofing powder added at the rate of 5 lb per cwt) to 3 parts of sharp sand, thoroughly mixed, and with water added to form a stiff paste, and applied 1 inch thick.

When it has dried out the pond can (and should) be filled with water, but it cannot be stocked because of the disastrous effects on plants and fish of free lime which soaks out of the new concrete. One answer to this problem is to empty and refill the pond three times over a period of six weeks. A quicker solution is to paint the concrete with Silglaze, a colourless compound which seals off the harmful lime from contact with the water. In addition a liquid plastic paint may be used to add colour, but this seems a pointless expense because the natural colour and pleasing texture of the concrete is obscured and the colour soon disappears under a film of algae and sediment.

Pre-formed ponds
There is obviously a great saving in labour if, instead of fabricating the pond yourself, you buy one ready-made. A considerable range of designs is offered, in Britain at least. Some are made of resin-bonded

glassfibre, which means that they are extremely strong and durable and also relatively expensive. Others, moulded in less rigid plastics, are cheaper and more vulnerable to damage. Propped against the garden centre fence they manage to give an impression of size which proves misleading when they are sunk into the ground. Their designers clearly fell into the trap of trying to achieve 'interesting' shapes. Pinched-in waists and indented edges abound: only one or two have a reasonably open shape. Indeed the vast majority of ready-made ponds fall so far short of the ideal specification that, except for the largest, they can be eliminated from serious consideration. Many are too small and too shallow to be fit for anything but birdbaths, as yet very few are deeper than 18 inches, and most have a poor volume/surface area ratio. They may conceivably be employed in a subordinate role, as reserve ponds for rearing fish fry or *Daphnia*, and the cheaper moulded ponds are just the thing if children want to keep newts, frogs, spawn and tadpoles.

The installation of ready-made ponds is not difficult. A hole is excavated to the required depth, and a few inches larger all round than the pond shape. The pond is placed in position, on a firm base, and back-filled round the sides, care being taken to work soil under the shelves so that there is firm support at all points. Frequent use should be made of the spirit level.

A well-made glassfibre pond, although flexible enough to give under ice pressure with no fear of damage, is rigid enough to be installed half out of the ground. A hole is dug only large enough to contain the lower half, usually up to shelf level, so that the shelves rest conveniently on the ground surface. The above-ground part can be surrounded by a low wall, at a distance from the pond rim which can be conveniently covered by stone slabs. The space between wall and pond sides must be packed tight with soil (or can be filled with concrete). It is, of course, easier to do this with a rectangular pond than with one of irregular shape, and it is an arrangement particularly suited to a formal patio or courtyard setting. Part of the retaining wall might be built up an extra 6 inches or so to make a seat. An undoubted benefit of this type of installation is that wind-blown dust and leaves finish up at the base of the wall instead of in the water.

Pond liners

Polythene was the first sheet plastic to be used for pond-making. It worked well but was shortlived. It punctured easily and above water level it flaked and cracked after twelve months' exposure to ultra-violet light. There was no way of repairing it. Nevertheless it was cheap and it had its uses. It does still, where a temporary pool is needed. Blue or black polythene has better resistance to ultra-violet, and a double layer of 500 gauge gives a better safety margin than a single, thicker, sheet.

If polythene had no future for the construction of large permanent water garden features, at least it hinted that the time would come when a hole in the ground could be given a waterproof lining without turning a single spadeful of concrete. It was only a question of finding stronger flexible sheets. They turned up in the form of laminated PVC and synthetic rubber, and in Britain, where this pond-making technique was pioneered in the early 1960s, far more ponds are now made with these materials than any other.

Butyl synthetic rubber sheet 0.030 inches thick is the Rolls-Royce of pond liners and, for my money, of all pond-making materials. Its charcoal black colour does not appeal to everyone at first sight. In practice it proves very satisfactory, giving an illusion of greater depth and improving reflecting quality. It makes a far more effective and natural background to the colour of plants and fish than any blue material. The life expectation of butyl is estimated at 50 to 100 years; for obvious reasons the proof of this claim lies some years distant.

For anyone not planning that far ahead, laminated PVC offers a proved material, at about half the cost of butyl, that should last 10 to 15 years, and perhaps more, if carefully installed. Black on one side and light brown on the other, it can be used either way up (black side up is recommended). There is a more expensive version of laminated PVC in which nylon or terylene net is incorporated to give extra strength. Certainly it has greater burst strength which would only be an advantage if the pond was hanging in the air on the end of a rope. In fact, the reinforced material, though doubtless valuable for other applications, offers no special benefits for the water garden.

Butyl rubber and laminated PVC are the viable alternatives. Both are simple and effective in use and both offer excellent value when cost is related to useful life. Draped in a hole and filled with water, each will mould itself faithfully to every contour of the excavation. They can be obtained in almost any size, giving the pond-maker freedom to design a feature that fulfils all the specified ideals of shape, size and profile and exactly suits the needs of his particular site. They also stretch and can thus absorb without harm the stresses resulting from ice pressure, or from soil movement, that are so often fatally damaging to a concrete pond. Accidents can happen, of course (I recall an icy path, beside a pond, taken by someone who happened to be carrying a garden fork ...) but both these materials are easily

21

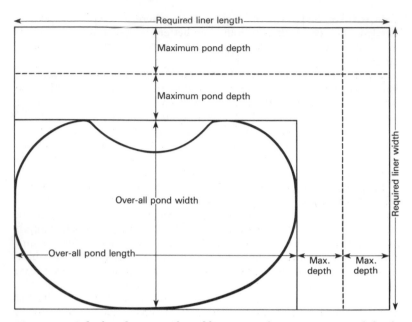

Figure 1   Calculate liner size by adding twice the maximum pond depth to both the length and width of the pond. Particularly with complicated shapes, take care to measure the over-all pond dimensions, i.e. the size of the smallest rectangle which will enclose the surface shape.

repairable (see pp. 138–9). An installation technique has been evolved which uses the stretch quality to minimise wrinkling.

To calculate the size of the liner needed it is first necessary to measure the over-all length and over-all width of the pond (see Figure 1); in effect, the size of the smallest rectangle which will enclose the surface shape. Twice the maximum pond depth is added to this length and width. For example, a pond 9 by 6 feet over-all and 18 inches deep would need a liner 9 + 3 by 6 + 3 = 12 by 9 feet. Reversing the procedure, possible pond sizes can be determined from a given liner size. Suppose you have a liner 16 by 12 feet, and plan on a depth of 2 feet. Subtracting twice the depth from the length and width of the liner shows that your pond can be any shape within a surface rectangle 12 by 8 feet.

It will be noticed that no allowance is made for a flap of spare material round the edge. This is not necessary because the slope on the pool walls and the stretch-fitting technique will automatically result in ample spare material to be secured under the surrounding paving or turf. If a non-stretching liner is used, such as polythene, then it is as well to add an extra foot to the dimensions of the calculated liner size. The presence or otherwise of marginal shelves does not affect these calculations.

Liner installation
Making a pond with butyl or PVC starts, as always, with the removal of 2 inches of soil over the area of pond plus surround, and levelling, before proceeding to excavate to the desired shape and profile including, of course, the shaping of any marginal shelves. Excavated soil must be moved away to leave at least 3 feet clear all round the hole. A simple template cut from hardboard (see Figure 2) is useful for checking wall slope and shelf depth. Anything that represents an obvious danger to the liner – sharp stones, broken pots or glass, bits of wire – must be removed and the floor and shelves given a covering of sand, sifted soil, peat, sawdust, old polythene fertiliser sacks, roofing felt, old carpet, bits of underfelt or several thicknesses of newspaper. Anything, in fact, which will form a smooth even bed for the liner. Only if the soil is flinty will it be advisable to trowel damp sand onto the sides, or cover them with some of the materials mentioned above. The excavation edge over which the liner will be drawn should always be given protective draping.

The liner is stretched over the hole, making sure the overlap is even all round, and the edges weighted with bricks or spaced bits of paving. The weight must be over the liner edge, not the edge of the

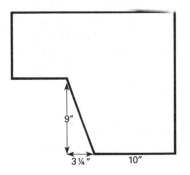

Figure 2   Hardboard template for checking simultaneously the depth, width and level of the marginal shelf, and the angle of wall slope.

hole. The liner will not be stretched taut: it will sag, and with butyl there is no harm if its weight makes it sag to touch the bottom. No attempt, however, should be made to shape it over the shelves or push it into corners: let the water do that. Turn a hose onto the sheet, and see how the weight of water gradually stretches the liner down, spreads it across the bottom and, as the water rises, moulds it up the walls and over the shelves. In the later stages alternate weights may be removed from the edges to allow some creep inwards but there should always be some tension so that wrinkling on curves is kept to a minimum. Some wrinkling is unavoidable since a two-dimensional sheet is being adapted to a three-dimensional shape, but it will barely be noticeable when the pool is stocked. When the pond is full – and it will take hours if it is a reasonable size – the remaining anchor weights are removed and any surplus liner trimmed off to leave a flap about 6 inches wide all round. Save the trimmed-off bits, incidentally: they might have a use later (see p. 138). Wrinkles in the flap can be nicked to allow it to lie flat.

Finishing the Edge
Paving is bedded on a mixture of 1 part cement to 3 of sand on top of the flap. Try to avoid getting much of the mix in the water: if a lot falls in, the water will have to be changed before stocking. It is important to project the paving 2 inches over the water and this in turn means that small pieces are useless. The first visitor who stands on the edge may find himself abruptly unbalanced. Large, or at least long, pieces are necessary to project the desired 2 inches and still reach far enough back from the edge to ensure stability.

In loose soil the edges of the excavation may tend to crumble; if so, it is advisable to create a hard edge to give the paving firm support. The method is illustrated in Figure 3.

Turf can be carried right to the water's edge along part of the pool perimeter, if desired, but it must be the side that will get least foot traffic. On this side the flap of spare liner must not be laid flat but turned down at 45° and buried so that the grass has soil to root into. Let the turf bend over the edge just to touch the water, leaving no liner exposed to the sun.

Refinements
If, at a future stage, it is intended that a submersible pump will be used to supply a waterfall, some thought should be given to its likely position. The pump will be close to the waterfall, and its cable will, if simply led up and over the edge of the paving, be unsightly and

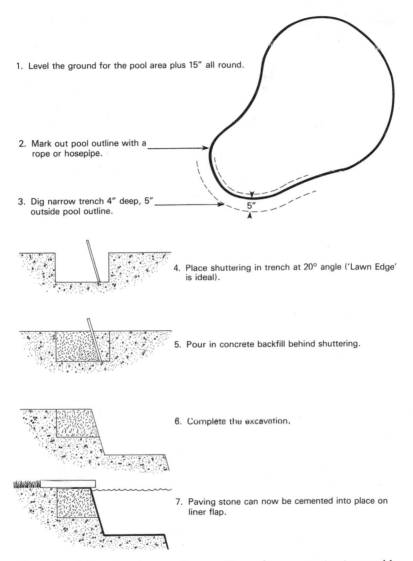

1. Level the ground for the pool area plus 15″ all round.

2. Mark out pool outline with a rope or hosepipe.

3. Dig narrow trench 4″ deep, 5″ outside pool outline.

5″

4. Place shuttering in trench at 20° angle ('Lawn Edge' is ideal).

5. Pour in concrete backfill behind shuttering.

6. Complete the excavation.

7. Paving stone can now be cemented into place on liner flap.

Figure 3   Collapsing edges can be a problem when excavating in crumbly soil. Here is a method of creating a firm edge and solid support for paving stones that will not tilt.

25

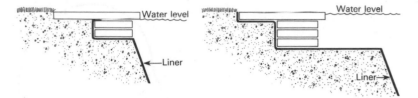

Figure 4 If the liner is taken behind bricks or stone slabs it will not be exposed to view—or to the effects of ultra-violet light—even if the water level drops several inches. Such an arrangement also provides very firm support for the paving finish. The brick/stone buttress can be built up from shelf level as shown in the sketch on the right; it also shows how to achieve the highest possible water level by taking the liner round the back edge of the paving to finish at ground level.

possibly hazardous. In addition, a length of $\frac{3}{4}$-inch (at least) delivery hose will reach from the pump to the top of the watercourse. So, beneath whichever paving slab in the surround you estimate will be handiest (if there is room over the liner flap), or between pairs of paving stones, embed two lengths of $\frac{3}{4}$-inch i.d. plastic hose, one for the cable to pass through, the other to be connected in due course to more hose conveying water to the fall. If it never happens, not much will have been lost anyway.

An absolutely level pond, kept well filled, will leave very little of the liner exposed above the waterline and that little will be shaded from exposure to ultra-violet light by the projecting paving stones. This is an important factor in prolonging the liner's useful life. With a little extra trouble it is possible to ensure that even if the water level drops several inches the liner will still not be exposed either to view or to the effects of sunlight. This involves taking the liner horizontally under, or between, paving slabs several inches below water level, then up behind the buried ends of the slab(s). This is clearly illustrated in Figure 4.

Whereas areas of shallow water are generally to be avoided, a shelving pebbled-beach effect can make a visually agreeable feature in a large water garden layout. The liner in the chosen area should slope at about 20 degrees to the horizontal and briefly become quite horizontal before dropping steeply to the pool floor. The shallows will need to stretch several feet to look effective. The largest pebbles that can be found are then laid in a single layer to cover the slope, with a line of stone slabs along the horizontal lower edge to make sure that none roll down into the deep. Be warned that algae will proliferate in these shallows, it will be less prolific if the 'beach' slope faces north

Bog Garden

An area for bog plants can be created within the pool perimeter by making a wide shallow slope (as for the pebble beach) and covering it with soil which will climb out of the water but always, of course, be very moist. A retaining wall will be needed to keep the soil in place but there will always be some risk of muddying. It is not an arrangement that I particularly like. It is better, I think, if the bog garden, though close to the pond, is not an integral part of it. Its desirability, and its construction, are discussed as a separate item in Chapter 6.

Availability

Laminated PVC and butyl rubber pond liners are available off the shelf at most British garden centres, in a convenient range of standard sizes under a variety of brand names. Specialist water garden suppliers can produce almost any required non-standard size to order in PVC or butyl – but check that the butyl is not less than 0.03 inches thick. Both materials are fairly widely available in Europe too, but in the USA they are, surprisingly, difficult to find. However, there seem to be feasible alternatives. There is Hypalon, a black material used for the creation of reservoirs and farm water storage ponds, and there are swimming pool liners. These materials, I understand, do not stretch, which means that, like polythene, they cannot be installed by the stretch-fitting technique, but must be well tucked into the excavation before water is run in, and folded and smoothed as the water rises. A new flexible sheet known as CPE should prove a boon to water gardeners if it really is, as claimed, impervious to the effects of ultra-violet light, but at the moment it can only be mentioned as seeming to be a promising subject for future experiment. Fortunately there are signs that it may not be too long before butyl rubber liners (or a 70 : 30 blend of butyl and EPDM, which is highly satisfactory) are available from at least some US water garden specialists.

Curing

When a moulded plastic pond, or one made with sheet plastic, is filled, it is in theory ready for immediate stocking, unless it is completed before plants are seasonally available. Certainly there are no curing problems, as with concrete, but I think a week should be allowed to pass before there is any rush to stock it. After a week chlorine will have dispersed and the water will have assumed the pale amber tint that indicates the presence of innumerable microscopic life forms. Stocking can go ahead, first with plants and later, when the plants are established, with fish. If a fountain or waterfall is contemplated, however, there is still some constructional work to be done. Such a feature can certainly be added at a later stage, but now is the time to consider what is involved.

3
Fountains and Waterfalls

In hot weather the cooling sound of splashing water is a delight. There can hardly be a better way to dismiss the pressing problems of the world and recharge flattened batteries than relaxing by the pool, lulled by the murmur of moving water. The essence of this pleasurable sensation is, of course, sound; there is no point in moving the water about if it does not bubble and splash.

How will the occupants of the pool react to water movement? Fish will not be concerned with the sound but to them, too, mere currents are nothing; splashing water is what counts and they will revel in it. They like it because the mixing of air and water increases the amount of dissolved oxygen in the water, though not to any great extent. What is more important, though less generally realised, is that turbulence greatly increases the rate at which carbon dioxide is released from the water. This is refreshing for the fish at any time; in any circumstances that result in the water becoming heavily over-charged with carbon dioxide, the splash of a fountain or a waterfall can mean the difference to fish between life and death.

Water plants do not enjoy either splash or currents. Water lilies in particular respond best to warm static water. They will not thrive in cold water and strong currents or under the rain of a fountain spray that waterlogs a flower as soon as it opens. It is clear that water movement that makes a splash has some advantages, but it must not be overdone. It must be created by circulating the pond's own, sun-warmed water, and not by piping in a continuous flow of cold mains water. Things must be arranged so that streaming currents are not created across the pond. Currents that make no sound have no purpose; the splash is what matters.

This can be produced by either a fountain or a waterfall. I have never yet seen a pond in which both looked right together. It may simply be a personal prejudice, but it seems to me that the totally unnatural symmetry of a fountain spray needs to be matched with the geometrical symmetry of a circular or rectangular pool in a formal setting. Even there I would not use a fountain unless there was ample room for lilies to spread their leaves well out of reach of wind-drifted

This young Fantail Goldfish has black markings which will probably disappear as it gets older.

spray. Beside that same formal rectangular pool a pile of rock with a waterfall cascading down it would be an offence. What can be done to produce an acceptable splash in that situation? A spouting ornament is one possibility. A stone frog, perhaps, spouting a thin arc of water; not too much volume, but a satisfactory splash that disturbs only a very small area of water. I recall also a memorable Chelsea Show exhibit, a formal garden with a large rectangular pool surrounded by paving and flower borders. On the paving at the side of the pool stood a wide-mouthed earthenware jar; a second jar lay beside it on the flags, and from its lip water poured endlessly into the pool fed, of course, by a skilfully concealed submersible pump. There was the desirable splash, depriving plants of very little space, ingeniously contrived to fit perfectly into the setting.

A waterfall imitates nature and goes perfectly with an informal pond provided that a low rockery will fit into the over-all garden design. A fountain there would destroy the natural effect. However, if fancy dictates both, it can be arranged easily enough.

Making a Waterfall

Water running down a slope, even a cobbled one, makes no worthwhile noise; it also happens to be the perfect way to grow sheets of slimy-looking filamentous algae, so it is an arrangement to be avoided. To make a lively splash it is necessary to make a watercourse in steps, so that the water has to fall clear from one step to the next. The length of the 'treads' and the height of the 'risers' in this staircase of water will depend entirely on the extent of the site and the angle of the slope. Generally, vertical drops of 6 to 12 inches are sufficient. Even a single fall of water into the pond is enough to make a perfectly adequate splash and it need not be more than a few inches high to be effective. Too small pools are overpowered by high waterfalls churning over far too much water for the plants ever to have a fair chance. Enough, here, is very much better than a feast.

Some of the soil excavated to make the pond can be used to build a flanking rockery (though it must be kept away from the pool side until liner installation is completed). If the site is flat a mountain will look absurd. Keep the soil mound low and wide with only enough stone to hint at a rocky outcrop. Most rockeries have far too much rock. Remember that a three-step series of falls need not rise higher than 18 inches above water level. Remember too that the higher the water has to be lifted the stronger the pump will have to be. Go much over 3 feet and there will be a substantial jump in the cost of a pump adequate to do the job. The width of the sill or lip over which water pours from one step to the next can also make a lot of difference. There must be enough water to pour cleanly without dribbling back, but at the same time volume must not be excessive. A flow of 300 gallons per hour will pour over a 3-inch wide sill about $\frac{1}{2}$-inch deep; over a 6-inch sill, $\frac{1}{4}$-inch deep; over a 12-inch sill it will be spread too thin to pour. A sill width of 3 to 6 inches is usually quite adequate, with a flow rate somewhere between 50 gallons and 70 gallons per hour per inch of sill. To avoid disturbance to plants the total volume of water handled per hour should, ideally, be approximately the volume of water in the pool; twice the pond volume per hour is acceptable; and three times the pond volume per hour should never be exceeded. Thus, a pond containing 300 gallons of water will have, ideally, a waterfall flow rate of about 300 gph and this will permit sill widths between 4 and 6 inches.

The quick-and-easy method of making a watercourse in a rockery is to slap down concrete on hollows and channels scraped out between rockery stones. The invariable result is that the pond water level drops rapidly because most of the water pumped up never gets back to the pond. The reasons are usually too-thin concrete laid on loose soil which settles and causes cracks, generally at the junction of stone and concrete, where there is always seepage anyway, because a watertight bond between the two is not possible. The way to make a waterproof watercourse with concrete is first to consolidate the soil very thoroughly, then to lay a concrete shell that runs without a break from top to bottom. Rocks are cemented onto the basic shell to form the details of the watercourse but they must not penetrate through it. More simply, butyl rubber can be used, with stone cemented onto it, to form the underlying waterproof membrane that guarantees the return to the pond of all the water pumped up. The simplest way of all is to use pre-formed stream sections and cascade pools with pouring lips that are now widely available. The flimsier ones are difficult to disguise as anything but shiny plastic. Precast concrete units are much easier to disguise but heavy and awkward to handle. The best (and inevitably the most expensive) are moulded in glassfibre to imitate effectively the colour and texture of rockery stone. Firmly set in the soil, flanked and supported with natural stone, and edged with draping alpine plants and conifers, they make an efficient and natural-looking watercourse.

Choosing a pump
The best pump for a particular purpose can only be recommended when the purpose is precisely specified. I can only offer advice in general terms. For example, use a pump that is designed specifically for the purpose. Adaptations of central heating or washing machine pumps to water garden use are not a success. If the scheme is a simple one involving one fountain or waterfall, a perusal of catalogues should produce the answer. If the problem is more complex, or in any case of doubt, take advantage of the expertise of a water garden specialist; and make sure he has all the facts. Is the pump to supply a fountain, a fountain ornament, a waterfall, or a combination of several of these? Give him the volume of the pond, or at least its dimensions. In the case of a waterfall, what sill widths are contemplated, and what is the required lift, i.e. the vertical difference between the pond water level and the top of the watercourse? Given this information he can recommend the pump that will do the job most efficiently and economically. For a waterfall installation it will be one that produces volume rather than pressure; for fountains, pressure is needed rather than volume. The basic choice will be between a surface pump and a submersible.

Surface pumps

A surface pump is located outside the pool, but close to it. It must be mounted on blocks or board and housed in a weatherproof chamber to keep it dry. Damp damages surface pumps more often than anything else. The pump chamber must be thoroughly ventilated, and never lined with polythene. The pump should not be left switched off for long periods. The ideal position for the pump chamber is the one that keeps both suction and delivery (but particularly suction) hose as short as possible. A surface pump draws water from the pond through a strainer and suction hose then delivers it to fountain and/or waterfall outlets through PVC delivery hose.

On the suction side it is essential to use armoured or reinforced hose to avoid collapse under suction pressure. The suction hose must be of the correct size to ensure adequate water flow into the pump, and must never be smaller in diameter than the size recommended by the manufacturer. The collapse of unsuitable tubing, the use of inadequate-sized suction hose, a clogged strainer, or an impellor jammed with rubbish, can reduce water flow on the suction side, resulting in overheating and damage to the pump motor. The use of a thermal overload starter, which will switch off the motor if it overheats, can prevent this sort of damage, which is not likely to be covered by manufacturers' guarantees.

If a surface pump is mounted above water level, prime can be maintained when the pump is switched off only by the use of either a footvalve strainer (which must be vertically positioned or it will not work) or a priming tank holding 50 per cent more water than the volume contained in the suction pipe.

If the pump is installed below water level there will be no priming problem, but there will be a risk of water from the pond flooding the pump chamber if there are any leaks in the pipework. Whether the pump is above or below water level it is vital that all joints between pump and hose and strainer are made completely airtight and watertight by the use of jubilee clips. Air sucked in through bad joints is a common cause of loss of prime and poor pump performance.

On the delivery side there can be any number of outlets of any size within the capacity of the pump. For delivery to fountains $\frac{1}{2}$-inch diameter hose is adequate; delivery hose to waterfalls may be $\frac{3}{4}$-inch or larger, depending on the pump size. Over long distances, hose diameter may need to be increased to compensate for friction loss. As a very rough guide, one foot of head will be lost for every 10 feet of pipe run.

Control valves restricting water flow on the delivery side will do the pump no harm. It is only on the suction side that the reduction of water flow is dangerous.

Submersible pumps
A submersible pump is designed to operate in water, and most models will suffer damage if they are not always completely immersed. The pump simply sits in the pond, needing no pump chamber and not a great deal in the way of plumbing. It may have a fountain jet mounted directly on top. Alternatively (or additionally in some cases) it can supply a waterfall, or $\frac{1}{2}$-inch hose can connect it to a fountain ornament. The pump should not sit on the bottom where it is likely to be clogged by silt and debris. It may be raised on bricks or placed on a shelf, provided there is enough water to cover it. If filter clogging continues to be a problem, the pump can be buried in a container full of coarse gravel or pebbles: this will act as an effective coarse strainer without seriously interfering with water flow.

The installation of submersible pumps is relatively simple and for most small and medium-sized ponds they are the most economical means of water circulation. For large-scale effects there are submersibles of adequate performance but a surface pump of similar output may well prove to be substantially cheaper.

Siting and connection
Strong currents, as already noted, have an inhibiting effect on water lilies. They can be avoided, or at least limited in their extent, by care in positioning the pump. The secret is to arrange things so that the point at which water is drawn from the pool is as close as possible to where it returns. It is of little significance where fountains are concerned but important in the case of waterfalls, because of the water volume involved. A submersible pump supplying a waterfall should be as close as possible to the point where water pours back into the pool, thus minimising the area of disturbance. In the case of a surface pump the strainer will be as close as is practicable to the waterfall and, in the interest of keeping the suction hose as short as possible, the pump chamber will need to be reasonably close to the waterfall too. If water is taken from the pool at the opposite end to the waterfall the length of either suction or delivery hose must be greatly increased, with a serious effect on efficiency and output, and currents will stream down the length of the pool, to the detriment of the lilies.

All pumps are electrically powered. Most submersibles operate on mains voltage, but some are low-voltage units supplied with a mains isolating transformer. Even with the latter, mains voltage runs along the cable connecting the transformer to the power source. Whatever length has to be joined, the cable sealed into the pump should for safety's sake be armoured cable. If several connections are required (for pumps, lights, heater) a waterproof junction box to provide terminals near the pool will be worthwhile. So will switches in or near the house to provide remote control of the moving water and lighting display.

Pump failure

It is only realistic to recognise the possibility that a pump, like any other mechanical device, may break down. Unless it is motor failure in one of the small submersibles in which the motor is inaccessible the pump will, with any luck, be repairable. But for a time the pond will be without a pump and the fountain or waterfall it supplies. This possibility should be borne in mind when the time comes to work out how many fish the pond will hold (see p. 118). I have every sympathy for the fish and none at all for the fish-keeper when I hear someone lament that his fish are dying because his pump has broken down. He should not have kept on adding fish to the point where their survival depended entirely on the continued functioning of a pump.

Lighting

Moving water, more than any other garden feature, makes the use of lighting well worth while. This is particularly the case when fountains and waterfalls are illuminated by underwater lights. Remarkably beautiful effects are produced when a lamp is placed below and behind the curtain of water pouring down from the fall; or by two or three lamps, perhaps of different colours, shining upwards through the crinoline of a fountain spray pattern. It is absolutely essential, of course, to use only lighting specifically designed for use in water. Whatever you do, do not flood the pool with light from a lamp in the nearest tree. That will kill the effect of the underwater lights completely.

4
Plants

At this point it is assumed that constructional work is complete and a new pond lies empty and ready for stocking. The first impulse is to put in a few fish, just to see some life in it. This impulse must be resisted, as far as goldfish are concerned anyway, because their presence will make it impossible to get certain essential plants established. Oxygenators must have time to get settled in without harassment; only when they are well rooted and growing away strongly will they be able to shrug off damage by nibbling fish. I believe in giving the oxygenators about 4 weeks' start. If there is a lot of family pressure for just a few fish a solution is to put in some small Golden Orfe. They are insect eaters and will not bother the plants. They will eliminate any mosquito that tries to colonise the pond, and provide some colour and lively movement. Be firm, however: only a few small ones and absolutely no goldfish, shubunkins or other members of the carp family for another month.

In making a selection of plants there are two things to look for. One is ornamental quality; the other is practical value, particularly in achieving that elusive target of permanently clear water generally referred to as pond balance. It is the fact that they possess both these qualities to a very high degree that makes water lilies supremely important. They produce superb flowers over a long season. Their spreading leaves, by cutting off sunlight and shading the water beneath, are the crucial factor in keeping the water clear. This function is more important, I am convinced, even than that of the oxygenating plants which usually get all the credit.

There are hardy water lilies and tropicals. The tropical lilies can be grown outside the tropics but only, with any real success, in areas where night temperatures in the summer are consistently warm. This includes much of the United States, parts of Australia and New Zealand, and southern Europe. In Britain they can be splendid under glass, but seldom, alas, outdoors.

Hardy lilies will grow almost everywhere and need no winter protection unless there is a danger of the soil they are growing in freezing solid. Certainly they do not need to be coddled in Britain.

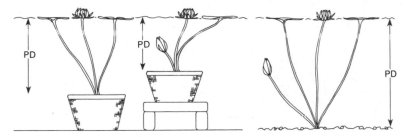

Figure 5   Planting depth (PD) refers always to the distance from the water surface to soil level, whether the soil is the bottom of a natural pond or in a planting basket.

They are perennial in the colder latitudes, flowering from June to October and becoming dormant in winter. In warmer climates they flower longer and in some places never seem to stop growing. They are planted only while in active growth, never when they are dormant.

Since hardy lilies are for obvious reasons of far wider interest than tropicals, they receive the greatest emphasis in the listing that follows. The problem of which varieties to include was resolved largely by reference to what nurseries around the world offer in their catalogues. It has meant leaving out a few temperamental beauties, but there is little point in including a variety that has been much praised in the past if nobody is now offering it for sale.

The guide to selection based on colour and classifications of vigour is an attempt to simplify matters for the novice water gardener. It can, of course, deal only in approximations. Fine gradations of colour cannot be represented; and the infinite variations in vigour and leaf spread, not only between one variety and another but also between plants of the same variety grown in different soils and climates, simply cannot be neatly sorted into pigeonholes. Nevertheless, if studied in conjunction with the colour plates and the varietal descriptions, it may help to resolve some of the problems of choice.

It will be seen that pond depths of 18 to 24 inches, giving a planting depth of 10 to 16 inches (8 inches being allowed for soil, which is not included in the term 'planting depth' – see Figure 5), make comfortable quarters for most of the lilies in the chart. The smallest can always be accommodated by raising their containers on a brick or two. Numbers are determined by pond area. Assuming a pond of 50 square feet surface area, and the advisability of covering

Hardy Water Lilies

A guide to selection according to colour, planting depth, and surface coverage.

Planting Depth	Red	Pink	White	Yellow and 'Sunset'	Approx. Surface Cover	
					Spread	Area
Group 1 3–9″ (8–25 cm)	*pygmaea rubra*	Joanne Pring	*pygmaea alba*	*pygmaea helvola*	1¼ ft (0.4 m)	0.14 sq yd (0.11 sq m)
Group II 5–12″ (13–30 cm)	Ellisiana	*laydekeri lilacea*	Candida *odorata minor*	Aurora Paul Hariot	2 ft (0.6 m)	0.35 sq yd (0.29 sq m)
Group III 7–15″ (18–40 cm)	Froebeli *laydekeri fulgens* *laydekeri purpurata*	Mary Patricia Pink Opal Somptuosa	Hermine	Comanche Graziella	3 ft (0.9 m)	0.8 sq yd (0.66 sq m)
Group IV 9–18″ (25–45 cm)	James Brydon Lucida Gloriosa	Odalisque Helen Fowler Lustrous Rose Arey	Albatross Loose	Indiana *odorata sulphurea*	4 ft (1.2 m)	1.4 sq yd (1.2 sq m)

Planting Depth	Red	Pink	White	Yellow and 'Sunset'	Approx. Surface Cover	
					Spread	Area
Group V 9–24" (25–60 cm)	*atropurpurea* Wm. Falconer Newton Rene Gerard	Mme. Wilfron Gonnère Masaniello *odorata rosea* Pink Sensation	Gonnère Hal Miller *odorata alba*	Moorei Sunrise	5 ft (1.5 m)	2.2 sq yd (1.8 sq m)
Group VI 12–30" (30–75 cm)	Escarboucle Conqueror	Amabilis *marliacea carnea* *marliacea rosea*	Gloire de Temple-sur-Lot *marliacea albida* Virginalis	*marliacea chromatella*	6 ft (1.8 m)	3 sq yd (2.6 sq m)
Group VII 15–36" (40–90 cm)	Attraction Chas. de Meurville	Colossea Mrs Richmond *tuberosa rosea*	*alba* Gladstoniana *tuberosa richardsoni*	Col. A.J. Welch	8 ft (2.4 m)	5.6 sq yd (4.7 sq m)

N.B. Depth figures refer to water depth over the crown and do not include the depth of the soil layer or container in which the plant is grown. Spread can vary considerably according to the type of soil and planting method, and will be substantially reduced if the roots are in cramped containers.

half to two-thirds of it with foliage, then plants are needed to cover, at the most, 3.7 square yards. One from Group IV and one from Group V would do it; or four from Group III; or two from Group IV and one from Group III. Which ones are chosen from each section will depend on colour preferences and what takes your fancy among the pictures. Nature may well make nonsense of the mathematics, but crude and approximate as the groupings are, I think they can still offer useful pointers and perhaps avoid some of the more unhappy choices made by the inexperienced, particularly in burdening small ponds with grossly over-vigorous varieties.

The most vigorous are generally the easiest to propagate; they are also the ones most likely to be available in large quantities from lakes where they have been naturalised in the past. So cheap lilies are invariably vigorous lilies. And they look such good value compared to a smaller grower (which will inevitably be a smaller plant) at probably twice the price, and maybe more. In the long term, however, the smaller one may well prove better value, when it is purchased to replace the cheap vigorous one which swamped the pond and was eventually dug out and thrown away in disgust. Be wary; and be prepared to pay more for the right choice, remembering that it is not an annual. It will be there to give you increasing pleasure for many years to come.

One thing more: be wary, too, if a water gardener generously offers you a sturdy-looking lily root just to start you off. It may be from the goodness of his heart; or it may be that he has a good reason for wanting to get rid of it.

Hardy Water Lilies
In the following selection of hardy water lilies the number of the colour plate (where relevant) appears in bold type after the name, followed by the name and nationality of the raiser and, in Roman numerals, the size code. Refer to the selection guide for details of planting depth and surface spread.

Nymphaea alba. European species. Group VII.
Flowers white, 4–5 inches across; foliage green. Useful for cold deep water, still or sluggishly moving, where hybrids will not survive. Capable of developing, from shallow planting, into depths up to 10 feet. Not to be confused with (*marliacea*) *albida*.

Aflame: see Escarboucle.

Albatross (1). MARLIAC. French. Group IV.
Large white blooms with raised elongated petals like birds poised for flight. Purple-tinged young leaves mature to green.

Amabilis (5). MARLIAC. French. Group VI.
Flat, stellate, flowers up to 9 inches across mature from light salmon to rose pink. Sometimes called Pink Marvel.

atropurpurea (36). MARLIAC. French. Group V.
Rich crimson-purple flowers, 7–8 inches across, open wide (unlike the other dark red variety Wm. Falconer) to show off the golden eye of long curving stamens. Purplish young leaves become dark green.

Attraction (18 and 19). MARLIAC. French. Group VII.
A vigorous grower needing space to do itself justice. The pinky-white flowers common on young plants give little hint of the deep red richness of mature 8–10-inch blooms on established plants.

Aurora. MARLIAC. French. Group II.
The name is appropriate for a plant whose flowers go through such a rapid series of colour changes. Starting creamy yellow they become orange and finally dark red. Mottled foliage heightens the multi-coloured effect.

Candida (7). Species native to northern Europe and Asia. Group II.
An attractive lily with cup-shaped 3-inch white flowers that would be a more sensible choice for small ponds than the commonly used but very robust *marliacea albida*. Candida adapts well to tub culture.

Charles de Meurville (34). MARLIAC. French. Group VII.
A very robust grower with nicely proportioned burgundy-red 9-inch blooms and massive leaves.

Colonel A.J. Welch. MARLIAC. French. Group VII.
Yellow flowers are held well above the surface – but they are too few in relation to the mass of foliage. For use only in water too deep for the other yellow varieties, all of which are superior. Leaves are only faintly marbled.

Colossea. MARLIAC. French. Group VII.
Usually listed as a pink, and certainly the 8-inch flowers have a tinge of flesh pink at first. This is quickly lost as the flower matures and the over-all effect is emphatically white. Flowers freely throughout the summer.

Comanche (6). MARLIAC. French. Group III.
The 4—5-inch flowers, held several inches above the surface, deepen from pinkish apricot to a coppery orange that is not quite red. Purplish young leaves become green speckled with brown.

Conqueror (28). MARLIAC. French. Group VI.
A good deep red variety that produces a lot of flowers and needs less space than the somewhat similar Attraction.

Crystal White: see Gonnère.

Ellisiana. MARLIAC. French. Group II.
A gem for small ponds and tubs. The $3-3\frac{1}{2}$-inch flowers are rich dark red deepening to purple at the centre. It is a little smaller than Froebeli but has more petals. A rarity worth searching for.

Escarboucle (4). MARLIAC. French. Group VI.
By general consent the best, brightest and most beautiful of all the reds; some rate it best among all the hardy lilies in its combination of flower quantity with superb quality. Also called Aflame.

Froebeli (24). FROEBEL. Swiss. Group III.
A very free-flowering and reliable small lily with deep red flowers; an ideal choice for small ponds and tubs.

Gladstoniana (37). RICHARDSON. American. Group VII.
Essentially a lily for large areas of water, preferably not less than 2 feet deep if the foliage is not to push above the surface and obscure the superb 8-inch white flowers.

Gloire de Temple-sur-Lot. MARLIAC. French. Group VI.
Crowded narrow incurving petals, blush pink at first changing to pure white, create the impression of waterborne chrysanthemums, and make this rare variety unique.

Gloriosa (20). MARLIAC. French. Group IV.
Bright red 6—7-inch blooms very freely produced, plus modest growth and relatively small leaf spread, make this the most popular red variety in the United States. It deserves to be more widely known in Britain.

Gonnère (25). MARLIAC. French. Group V.
One alternative name is Crystal White. Another is Snowball, even more appropriate in view of the 5—6-inch petal-packed globular snow-white flowers. Like James Brydon, whose carmine flowers are rather similar in shape, Gonnère has only a modest leaf spread. The two varieties look well together.

Graziella (27). MARLIAC. French. Group III.
A free-flowering lily whose 2–3-inch blooms are alleged to fade with age; I find its orange colour pretty consistent from the first day to the last.

Hal Miller. MILLER. American. Group V.
This recent hybrid, a cross between Virginalis and Sunrise, has very beautiful large creamy white flowers held above the surface, creating exquisite reflections.

Helen Fowler (33). SHAW. American. Group IV.
Among the finest of the *N. odorata* derivatives, this beautiful lily is now listed in surprisingly few catalogues. It has large rose-pink scented flowers held well above the surface and its leaf spread is modest.

Hermine. MARLIAC. French. Group III.
Attractive star-shaped white flowers stand 3 or 4 inches out of the water above green pads. Flowers profusely over a long season.

Indiana. MARLIAC. French. Group IV.
Another of the colour-changing 'sunset' group. In this one delicate orange-pink ages to coppery red. The leaves are heavily marked with purple.

James Brydon (15). DREER. American. Group IV.
Unquestionably one of the best, on several counts. The flowers, freely produced, are floating 5–6-inch bowls of rich carmine red. The leaves, bronzy purple to dark green, cover a remarkably small area of the surface. It can make do with less sun than most varieties. It is ideal for small pools, robust enough to hold its own in large ones, and ready to adapt even to the confines of a tub.

Joanne Pring. PRING. American. Group I.
A beautiful miniature lily with 2-inch deep pink flowers paling at the petal tip. Perfect for sinks and shallow tubs.

laydekeri fulgens (21). MARLIAC. French. Group III.
This and the following members of the *laydekeri* group are an ideal choice for small ponds and tubs, and, for that matter, any pond 18 inches deep (allowing 6 inches for the container depth and 12 inches of water over it) whatever its surface area. Their leaf spread is restrained and their flower production rate extravagant. *N. laydekeri fulgens* is rich red maturing to dark red, the flowers up to 4 inches across. Where lilies are grown *en masse l. fulgens* stands out at a distance as the brightest, most vivid red of all.

laydekeri lilacea (22). MARLIAC. French. Group II.
Slightly smaller than *l. fulgens* in growth, and with $2\frac{1}{2}$–3-inch, more cup-shaped flowers, rosy lilac maturing to carmine. The leaves, as with the rest of the group, are a uniform dark green.

laydekeri purpurata (23). MARLIAC. French. Group III.
A little larger in leaf than the two preceding but still adaptable to tub as well as pond culture. The rosy crimson flowers are larger too, though not quite as neat in shape, and produced in steady profusion through the season.

Loose. Origin unknown. American. Group IV.
Fragrant, 6-inch, snow-white, star-shaped flowers held almost a foot above the surface give this beautiful lily a tropical look: but it is definitely a hardy lily, and one of the best too.

Lucida (29). MARLIAC. French. Group IV.
A moderate grower, generous with its dark centred vermilion red blooms. The leaves are boldly patterned with purple.

Lustrous. Origin unknown. American. Group IV.
A compact grower with prolific blooms of great beauty. The broad petals are evenly coloured rose pink with the sheen of satin, the insides of the sepals a deeper pink.

Mme. Wilfron Gonnère (17). MARLIAC. French. Group V.
A beautiful lily with large pink double flowers; plain green leaves.

Marliac flesh: see *marliacea carnea.*

Marliac pink and Marliac rose: see *marliacea rosea.*

Marliac white: see *marliacea albida.*

Marliac yellow: see *marliacea chromatella.*

marliacea albida (12). MARLIAC. French. Group VI.
Large white flowers with golden centres: the dark green leaves are tinged with brown at the edges. Beautiful, reliable, as foolproof as a plant can be and invariably the cheapest hardy hybrid available, *albida* must be the world's most frequently planted lily. Often, regrettably, in tiny ponds too cramped for its lusty growth.

The fact that Marliac bestowed his own name on a group of hybrids strongly suggests that he regarded them as a major achievement. This variety, and the three following, all robust, free-flowering and virtually indestructable, have been the mainstay of water garden planting schemes for almost a century.

marliacea carnea (13). MARLIAC. French. Group VI.
This is always catalogued as a pink variety and the 7–8-inch flowers
on established plants do have a rosy flush at the base of the petals.
The over-all effect, however, is much more white than pink. Also
known as Morning Glory.

marliacea chromatella (14). MARLIAC. French. Group VI.
The popular name Golden Cup aptly describes the 6–7-inch creamy-
yellow flowers. Growth is vigorous and the large leaves are mottled
with chestnut.

marliacea rosea. MARLIAC. French. Group VI.
Hardly more than blush pink at first but when the plant is established
the classically shaped flowers are rose pink deepening towards the
centre.

Mary Patricia. JOHNSON. American. Group III.
A delightful small pond and tub lily which produces dainty, cup-
shaped, light pink flowers with great freedom.

Masaniello (30). MARLIAC. French. Group V.
A strong-growing free-flowering variety with large flowers. The
colour is a rose pink shading from pale in the outer petals to deep at
the centre and intensifying as the bloom matures.

Moorei. ADELAIDE BOTANIC GARDENS. Australian. Group V.
Primrose yellow blooms about 6 inches across. Distinguished from
marliacea chromatella chiefly by brown spotting rather than blotching
of leaves, and more restrained growth.

Morning Glory: see *marliacea carnea.*

Mrs Richmond (8). MARLIAC. French. Group VII.
A vigorous, prolific and very beautiful lily with 9-inch blooms, rich
pink deepening to carmine.

Newton (3). MARLIAC. French. Group V.
The flowers are vermilion red bowls half filled with unusually long
golden stamens and they are often lifted well above the surface,
making this a particularly attractive variety.

Odalisque (2). MARLIAC. French. Group IV.
Another that lifts its flowers inches above the water surface, with
reflexed sepals and outer petals. The colour shades with age from
deep rose to creamy pink.

odorata. North American species.
This fragrant species with 3–5-inch white blooms (often catalogued as *odorata alba*), and the deep pink *odorata rosea*, are ideal for lake margins where there is ample room to spread in relatively shallow water. *N. odorata* has given rise to many natural varieties and man-made hybrids.

odorata minor. Natural form. Group II.
A dwarf lily with pure white scented blooms 2–3 inches across and green leaves, red beneath, 3–5 inches in diameter.

odorata sulphurea grandiflora. MARLIAC. French. Group IV.
A fine yellow variety not dissimilar to *marliacea chromatella* in flower size and colour but quite different in character due to narrower and more numerous petals and the lifting of the flower well above the surface. The leaves are marbled above and red-spotted beneath.

Paul Hariot (26). MARLIAC. French. Group II.
A free flowering small grower with relatively large (up to 5 or 6-inch) blooms whose colour develops from buff yellow through orange pink to a deep pink, red at the centre.

Pink Marvel: see Amabilis.

Pink Opal. FOWLER. American. Group III.
Broad-petalled fragrant flowers, a unique shade of uniform rich pink that is almost light red. An outstanding variety for small ponds and tubs.

Pink Sensation. SLOCUM. American. Group V.
A recent hybrid of exceptional quality. The 8-inch blooms, evenly coloured rich silvery pink, are held well above the surface and remain open unusually late in the day. Very free-flowering.

pygmaea alba. Natural sport of *N.* Candida. Group I.
A charming white-flowered dwarf lily, ideal for tubs, sinks and small shallow pools.

pygmaea helvola. MARLIAC. French. Group I.
The perfect miniature. Numerous dainty star-shaped pale yellow blooms are matched by proportionately small mottled leaves.

pygmaea rubra. Probably a natural hybrid. Group I.
Slightly larger in leaf and flower than the other 'pygmies'. The blooms open pale pink and age to dark red. Foliage green.

Rene Gerard (32). MARLIAC. French. Group V.
A free-flowering variety of moderate leaf growth with proportionately large (9-inch) flowers. The substantial petals are pointed: colour develops from crimson-streaked pink to carmine red, darkest towards the centre.

Rose Arey (31). FOWLER. American. Group IV.
The 8-inch blooms are brilliant pink, the long pointed petals slightly rolled and incurved. Free-flowering when established, this elegant beauty is one of the most desirable of all hardy lilies.

Snowball: see Gonnère.

Somptuosa. MARLIAC. French. Group III.
A relatively compact grower with 5-inch cup-shaped double flowers, rose pink deepening at the centre to strawberry.

Sunrise (16). Origin uncertain, probably American. Group V.
A superb yellow lily with numerous narrow curving petals lifted well above the surface. The flowers have some scent and may be 10 inches or more across. Not all the plants sold under this name are correct. The true Sunrise has dark green leaves whose undersides are reddish marked with brown; the stems of leaves and flowers are clothed in fine hairs.

tuberosa richardsoni. RICHARDSON. American. Group VII.
Something of a giant, best suited to natural ponds and lakes where it can extend from a depth of 2 or 3 feet into even deeper water. The double globular white blooms may be 6–8 inches across.

tuberosa rosea. Natural hybrid. American. Group VII.
The pink flowers 4–5 inches across are fragrant and lifted above the surface, suggesting _N. odorata_ as one parent. Like the last, deepish water and plenty of elbow room are desirable.

Virginalis. MARLIAC. French. Group VI.
A beautifully proportioned flower considered by some to be the best of all the whites. It produces blooms very freely throughout a long flowering season.

William Falconer (35). DREER. American. Group V.
The very dark red of the 6–7-inch flowers invites comparison with _atropurpurea_. Difference lies not so much in colour as in flower shape: the blooms of _atropurpurea_ open wide to a saucer shape while more upright petals make cup-shaped a suitable description for Wm. Falconer.

Other Surfacing Plants

Surfacing plants, meaning those that root in soil and produce leaves and flowers on or just above the surface, include the invaluable water lilies, but few other hardy plants of real ornamental value.

Nuphars, though broadly similar to the *Nymphaea*, are altogether lacking in elegance and charm. With large thick leaves pushing above the surface and small thick-stemmed flowers, the best *Nuphar* is inferior even to the poorest of the hardy hybrid lilies. The European species, *Nuphar luteum*, and its North American counterpart, *N. advenum*, will grow well in shade, but the globular 2-inch yellow flowers occur freely only in the sun. They will succeed in moving water 6 feet deep or more and it is only in such situations, where hybrid lilies have no chance, that they have any value. They are much too vigorous for small ponds. *Nuphar japonicum rubrotinctum* is easily the best of the family; it has orange-scarlet flowers and erect dark green copper-burnished leaves. *N. japonicum variegatum* has leaves splashed with creamy white. The *N. japonicum* varieties need still water. *Nuphar pumila (minimum)* is a dwarf form suitable for small ponds and even aquariums.

Nymphoides peltata (**44**), a plant that has suffered several name changes, will be more familiar to many gardeners as *Villarsia nymphoides*, or Water Fringe. It looks like a miniature water lily with 3-inch floating leaves and dainty yellow flowers held clear of the surface. Its runners will speedily colonise any muddy shallows if it is not confined. 4–12 inches of water suit it best.

Orontium aquaticum, or Golden Club, has intriguing flower spikes that look like slender tapering white candles whose top few inches have been painted yellow. The bluey-green leaves stand erect or float according to the planting depth, which may be anything from 2 to 18 inches.

Aponogeton distachyus, or Water Hawthorn (**45**), is, apart from the lilies, easily the most valuable of the surfacing plants. Its flowers, curiously lobed and forked, are white with black anthers, and have more fragrance than any other aquatic plant. It flowers freely in early summer, just as freely again in the autumn, and sporadically through the rest of the year. Mild spells during the winter find it always ready to produce a few flower spikes, and over the years I have seen it in flower in every month. Allow the same space for it as a Group II lily, but do not be surprised if in time it occupies rather more, since it seeds readily. It can be started at any depth from 4 to 12 inches but will stand a lot more. A container of established *Aponogeton* that was nudged from a 2-foot level into a depth of 4 feet carried on as if nothing had happened. Destruction of the leaves by midge larvae can be almost total during midsummer but the plant responds with a healthy new set of foliage to go with the autumn crop of flowers. Even moderate shade does not discourage this obliging plant. There should be a place for it in every pond.

Submerged Oxygenating Plants

These are the plants that are commonly referred to in the United States as oxygenating grasses. In Britain they are called water weeds more often than not, which is a poor reward for what are, in effect, the pond's valuable maids-of-all-work. They provide a spawning medium for fish and a hiding place for fry; they harbour astonishing numbers of food organisms and in addition are themselves a valuable part of a goldfish's diet. They also produce oxygen, of course. So do all the other plants in the pond, but those with leaves on or above the surface discharge it into the air; oxygenators release it directly into the water (only, however, under the influence of strong light). At night they produce not oxygen but carbon dioxide, and, since fish are using oxygen and producing carbon dioxide all the time, it is clear that the notion of so many oxygenators plus so many inches of fish producing a balanced oxygen/carbon dioxide exchange is a fallacy. In fact, in a pond with the sort of proportions that have been discussed, all the oxygen fish need will be supplied simply by the natural process of absorption through the water surface.

What makes oxygenating plants valuable is not the production of oxygen; that is, possibly, the least of their virtues. Oxygenators need nutrients to build up their rapid summer growth and they feed not through roots, which are primarily for anchorage, but by absorbing dissolved mineral salts directly from the water through their leaves and stems. In this they compete directly with algae which rely on the same food source. The algae, starved of light by the leaves of water lilies and starved of food by the competition of oxygenators, die and sink and the water clears. That is why oxygenators need to be present in some numbers from the beginning in a new pond filled with mineral rich tapwater even further enriched by minerals dissolving out of the soil in planting containers. The standard recommendation is one bunch for every 2 square feet of water surface area. I would be satisfied with one for every 3 square feet in pools up to 100 square feet; above that one for every 4 square feet until, beyond 500 square feet, I would reduce the rate to one for every 6 square feet.

It is often stated, by people who should know better, that oxygenators are 'just dropped in'. True, some of the drifting fragments will eventually root somewhere, but this is not the way to get growth going quickly. They need to be planted (with one exception) and methods will be described hereafter.

There are a dozen kinds of oxygenator, and the best is the one that makes itself at home in your pond and flourishes mightily. The only way to find out which that is is to plant a mixture of several kinds. Which is usually the most rampant? *Elodea canadensis*. Which makes the neatest carpet of short growth? *Elodea canadensis*. Both answers are true if the questions are asked two or three years apart. Growth is fast and furious in a new pond because of the mineral-rich environment, but as nutrients are consumed growth settles down to a more sedate level. *Elodea crispa* makes long dark green ropes of growth; *Potamogeton crispus* has bronzy crinkled leaves with a seaweedy look about them; *Myriophyllum spicatum* is invariably described as feathery. *Fontinalis* (Willow Moss) makes dark green compact clumps and likes to grow with its wiry roots attached to stone, brickwork, concrete or pebbles; it tolerates more shade than the rest. These have no flowers that a gardener would recognise, but two other oxygenators do. *Ranunculus aquatilis*, the Water Crowfoot, produces a mass of small white flowers just above the surface. *Hottonia palustris*, or Water Violet, raises spikes of pale lilac flowers. They are far from showy and the fresh light green foliage is what makes it worth growing, especially since it is at its freshest in late winter and in autumn. *Vallisneria spiralis* (Eel Grass or Tape Grass) and Cabomba are two oxygenators that grow well outdoors in many parts of the United States but do not flourish in Britain except in aquariums.

The one type that really can be 'just dropped in' is *Ceratophyllum*, or Hornwort. It produces a dense growth of foliage bristly enough to discourage browsing goldfish.

Floating Plants

All this group have in common is their ability to feed through roots suspended in water without any contact with soil. They vary greatly in form, character and ornamental value. By shading the water and using up nutrients they help in suppressing algae, and fish use the root masses of some as spawning mats.

Azolla caroliniana (Fairy Floating Moss) spreads a mosslike sheet on the surface varying in colour from dark green to dark red. It can be a pest in large pools where control by netting is impractical.

Eichhornia crassipes (Water Hyacinth) **(49)** has swollen leaf stems that make each plant a buoyant island of dark shiny green. It raises spikes of beautiful pale lavender flowers and trails lengthy root masses ideal for spawning fish. The showiest of the floaters in a favourable climate, it can also spread at such a prodigious rate as to become a serious nuisance. In the United States its interstate movement is prohibited. Britain does not have the climate for *Eichhornia*. It is safe out of doors only in the summer and even then a cold snap may blacken it. It is a far better greenhouse than pond plant.

Hydrocharis morsus-ranae (Frog-bit) is a pleasant little plant with bright green leaves and small white flowers, but its soft foliage is irresistible to snails. If it survives their attacks it drops resting buds to the bottom in the autumn and the rest of the plant disintegrates. The buds rise to the surface in June to start off new plants – if the pond has not been cleaned out in the meantime.

Lemna is the generic name of the Duckweed group, which includes some of the worst water garden pests. Only *Lemna trisulca*, the Ivy-leaved Duckweed, which remains submerged except for a short spell at the surface in summer, is worth having, and that has no ornamental value. *Lemna minor,* and all other species that make carpets of bright green on the surface, should never be introduced deliberately, however nourishing they may be as fishfood. Difficult enough to control in a small pond, duckweed can be nothing short of a disaster in a large one.

Pistia stratiotes (Water Lettuce) really does resemble a flat type of garden lettuce, but with leaves like felt. It needs a hot climate. Cold destroys it and in Britain it does not thrive outdoors even in the summer.

Stratiotes aloides (Water Soldier) is a floating plant only when it rises to the surface in summer to produce a white flower. The rest of the year is spent on the bottom where it roots in mud. The spiky cluster of long sword-shaped leaves resembles the top of a pineapple.

Trapa natans and *T. bicornis* (Water Chestnuts) have small overlapping triangular leaves making an attractive flat rosette on the surface. They are annuals relying on seed production for the next generation. In Britain they rarely produce seed.

Eliminating from this list floaters that only occasionally float, floaters that can be a menace, and floaters that are not hardy in Britain, there is not much left to contribute ornamental surface coverage in British ponds. This does not matter if adequate algae-suppressing surface shading is provided by such attractive plants as hardy water lilies, *Aponogeton* and *Nymphoides*.

Marginal Plants

Pond plants that stand ankle-deep in shallow water and lift their stems and flowers above it are collectively referred to as marginals. They are not essential since they make no contribution to pool balance. They earn their place by virtue of flower power or ornamental foliage. Some of them spread rapidly and confinement to planting containers or corner pockets, with one variety only in each container, is recommended. Planting in a trough where different varieties can intermingle allows the coarsest grower to swamp the rest; you end up with a solid mass of the least attractive variety. In the following descriptions PD indicates planting depth, i.e. depth of water over the soil or container.

Acorus calamus variegatus has 30-inch leaves striped green and creamy white. PD 0–2 inches.

Alisma parviflora has broad dark green leaves, deeply veined, and much-branched stems sprinkled with tiny white flowers. Height 12 to 15 inches. PD 2–4 inches.

Alisma plantago (Water Plantain) has large leaves, very small pinkish flowers, and a tendency to crowd the containers of other marginal plants with its seedlings. Height 24 inches. PD 0–6 inches.

Butomus umbellatus, the Flowering Rush, has tall stems with clusters of small red-centred pink flowers. PD 2–6 inches.

Calla palustris (Bog Arum) is a spreading grower about 6 inches high with shiny leaves and miniature 'arum-lily' spathes. PD 0–3 inches.

Caltha. Marsh Marigold, Kingcup and Waterblobs are common names of these invaluable early-flowering plants. Happiest with their crowns barely covered by water, they brighten the pond edge from March to May. *Caltha palustris* (39), with single shiny flowers, grows about a foot high. *C. palustris plena* (38) smothers a compact 9-inch mound of leaves with very double yellow blooms. *C.p. alba* is white. *C. polypetala*, up to 3 feet high, with large single yellow flowers, has a loose sprawling habit; it is ideal for large areas of muddy shallows.

Cyperus longus is a graceful 4-foot foliage plant capable of developing into substantial clumps. PD 2–6 inches.

Eriophorum (**40**) has 18-inch grassy stems flying pennants of silky white down from June to August. Aptly called Cotton Grass. PD 2–4 inches.

Glyceria spectabilis variegata is a vigorous plant with lax foliage striped green and cream, attractive throughout the growing season. Container planting is essential to curb expansion. Height 3 feet. PD 0–6 inches.

Houttuynia cordata has red stems, blue-green heart-shaped leaves and small flowers with white bracts. *H.c. plena* is the double form. Height 18 inches. PD 0–4 inches.

Iris laevigata (**42**), the lavender blue water iris, and its varieties form the main flowering feature in June. *I.l. alba* is white (**42**); *I.l. colchesteri* (**43**) is white mottled with rich blue; *I.l. atropurpurea* is deep blue, and *I.l.* Snowdrift is a double white. The best of the family, and for me the best of all marginals, is *Iris laevigata variegata*. In addition to the lavender blue flowers it has fans of sharply defined leaf variegations in green and cream that look as fresh in October as in March. *I.l.* Rose Queen (**48**) is unique in this group in having soft pink flowers. This and other pointers suggest that it is a hybrid with *I. kaempferi* blood; certainly it is happier with its roots barely covered than in the 2 to 4 inches of water preferred by the other *laevigata* forms. All grow 2 to 2½ feet.

Iris pseudacorus is the vigorous yellow flowered Common Flag, 3 feet or more in height. *I.p. variegatus* is a more compact form with similar flowers and green/yellow striped leaves. The variegation fades rapidly after midsummer. PD 2–6 inches.

Lobelia cardinalis (**46**), normally thought of as a border plant that needs winter protection, proves to be quite hardy in Britain in water up to 6 inches deep. It has reddish foliage and flowers of brilliant scarlet from August to October. Height 3 to 4 feet. PD 2–6 inches.

Lysichitum americanum produces impressive yellow spathes 2 feet high in April followed, in summer, by 4-foot leaves. *L. camtschatcense* has white hoods. Both enjoy deep, acid, boggy soil but can be container-grown in shallow water. PD 0–1 inch.

Menyanthes trifoliata (Bog Bean) is useful at the front edge of the pond where taller growers would spoil the view of the lilies. Short spikes of pink-tinted white flowers in May and June among foliage about 9 inches high. PD 0–3 inches.

Mimulus guttatus is the Monkey Flower, yellow with red spots, that most commercial growers still call *M. luteus*. It flowers cheerfully from June to September and seeds itself with abandon. Height 1 foot. PD 0 2 inches. *M. ringens* is a relative with smaller, lavender blue flowers. Height $1\frac{1}{2}$ feet. PD 2–4 inches.

Myosotis palustris. The Water Forget-me-not, with its sky blue flowers and sprawling habit is untidy but charming. This and the following plant are exceptions to the rule about not mixing different marginals. Either can share a container with an upright-growing species, clothing its lower stems to advantage. PD 0–2 inches.

Myriophyllum proserpinacoides (Parrot's Feather) is even more rambling than *Myosotis*, throwing up arching sprays of cool emerald green foliage a surprising distance from its roots. Grown together, the two make a thoroughly attractive tangle that can always be tidied by cutting back. PD 0–6 inches.

Peltandra virginica makes a bold clump of rich green, deeply-veined, broad-arrow foliage with slender green spathes. Height 2 feet. PD 0–3 inches.

Pontederia cordata (41) combines enough good points – lush shiny leaves, spikes of blue flowers, late flowering from July to September, and restrained growth – to make it highly desirable even though it is never really showy. Height $2\frac{1}{2}$ feet. PD 2–4 inches.

Ranunculus lingua grandiflora is a 3 foot tall aquatic Buttercup called Spearwort. Like *Glyceria* it is a takeover specialist whose delight in aggressive expansion requires the curb of container planting. PD 2–6 inches. *R. flammula* is a smaller (9 inch) relation, of no great decorative value.

Sagittaria sagittifolia (47) is called Arrowhead, because of the shape of its broad 3-pointed leaves. *S. japonica* has a golden boss to its 3-petalled single white flowers, and *S.j. plena* has very double flowers. PD 4–6 inches.

Saururus cernuus is called Lizard's Tail from the curving, tapered spike of creamy, white flowers; they are delicately scented. Height 2 feet. PD 0–2 inches.

Scirpus albescens has crowded 4–6 foot rushy stems vertically lined with green and cream. PD 4–6 inches.

Scirpus zebrinus (Porcupine Quill or Zebra Rush) is a striking foliage plant growing about 4 feet high. The 'quills' are alternately banded with green and white. If it reverts to plain green stems the variegation can be restored by splitting and replanting.

Typha. These are the plants that produce the big velvety brown 'pokers' beloved of flower arrangers. They are often called Bulrushes, which is incorrect: that name properly belongs to a *Scirpus*. The correct name (and a very good descriptive name too) is Reed Mace; in the United States they are known as Cat-tails. *Typha latifolia*, the 8-foot giant of the family, is out of scale except in really large water gardens. The narrow-leaved graceful 5–6-foot *T. angustifolia* is much more useful, but it should never be turned loose in a natural pond. For small pools the $1\frac{1}{2}$-foot *T. minima*, which has short plump bosses, is the ideal choice. Root restriction by container planting is essential for all *Typhas*. PD 3–6 inches.

Zantedeschia aethiopeca, the Arum Lily, makes a splendid pond plant, and, under 6 inches of water, can be left to winter outdoors in Britain. PD 6–12 inches.

Planting Season

The time to plant aquatics is when they are actively growing and that does not happen until warm spring weather has taken winter's chill off the water. It will depend where you live, of course. In Britain some aquatics will be moving and plantable in late April, the majority by mid-May and a few (*Hydrocharis*, *Sagittarias*, and pygmy lilies, for example) not until June. May to July is the main season but planting can continue until September. A very cold spring can delay the start by weeks, and there is no point at all in trying to rush things. The season starts when plants are growing, not according to a date on the calendar. In warmer climates the season may well start earlier and continue longer.

Planting Method

If maximum plant growth is the aim there is no doubt about which is the most effective way to grow aquatics. You cover the entire pool floor, and fill any marginal troughs, with 6 to 8 inches of rich soil. This will provide enough nutrients for years of exuberant growth, but time will reveal some drawbacks. The more aggressive reeds and rushes will spread like wildfire, swamping choicer varieties, and any patches of open water will disappear under a blanket of massive lily leaves. If water is visible at all it will be muddied by fish foraging on the bottom, and that is the only way you will know the fish are there.

55

Wading in the pond – and it is occasionally necessary – becomes something of an adventure; and, when the need to sort out the tangle cannot be ignored any longer, removing the mud and the carpet of roots proves a monumental task.

Such unhappy results can largely be avoided by confining plant roots to containers. There they can be given enough soil to grow adequately without going mad. It will have to be replaced more frequently than if the whole floor was covered but much less soil will be needed each time. Between containers there will be no soil; that limits the scope for rampant spreaders and means wading is easier and less likely to stir things up. In ponds made with liners, incidentally, barefoot wading is strongly recommended. Wearing waders or even plimsolls it is easy to tread a stone through the liner without knowing you have done it until the water level begins to drop. Barefoot you will feel the stone and automatically take the pressure off before any damage is done.

Containers
Large planting areas in large ponds can be formed of 3-course brick walls cemented to the floor. Never use cement blocks for this or any other purpose in the pond unless they have been treated with Silglaze or have been pre-soaked elsewhere for a month.

Movable containers are preferable to fixed ones, but remember that a bushel of soil is likely to weigh about a hundredweight without counting the weight of the container. Carrying handles are a great help. Almost any receptacle that will not disintegrate in water will serve the purpose, provided that it has not contained oily or chemical substances. Stout wooden (but not redwood) boxes, tubs, and half casks are fine; metal containers, except copper or freshly galvanised, will do; plastic tubs and bowls are splendid. Plastic buckets are tempting – the carrying handle is a great convenience – but they are not the right shape. Like conventional garden pots, whether plastic or clay, they have the wrong proportions for shallow-rooting lilies. A plastic washing-up bowl is very much better than a bucket of equal volume because it is wide and shallow. A bushel box 20 inches square and 6 inches deep is much better than one 14 inches square and 12 inches deep. A plastic laundry basket is ideal for big lilies.

Soil
The ideal soil for aquatics, and particularly lilies, is a heavy rich garden or pasture loam. Sandy soil and mud from natural ponds are equally useless. Clay (especially blue clay) is acceptable but needs at

56

Planting Container Sizes

Alternative container sizes which will provide the desirable soil volume for single plants, and for three-plant groups, in various lily categories.

To Accommodate		Depth Inches *	Alternative Shapes	
Type	Number		Square Side Inches or	Circle Diam. Inches
Hardy lilies	1 plant	5	6	7
Group I	3 plant group	5	10	11
(soil volume allowed	1 plant	3	8	9
2 quarts per plant)	3 plant group	3	14	16
Hardy lilies	1 plant	7	7	8
Group II	3 plant group	7	12	13
$\frac{1}{8}$ bushel (4 quarts)	1 plant	5	8	9
per plant	3 plant group	5	14	16
Hardy lilies	1 plant	9	8	9
Group III	3 plant group	9	14	16
$\frac{1}{4}$ bushel (8 quarts)	1 plant	6	11	12
per plant	3 plant group	6	18	21
Hardy lilies	1 plant	9	12	13
Groups IV and V	3 plant group	9	20	23
$\frac{1}{2}$ bushel (16 quarts)	1 plant	6	15	17
per plant	3 plant group	6	26	29
Hardy, Group VI	1 plant	9	14	16
Tropical with	3 plant group	9	25	28
manure/fertiliser.	1 plant	6	18	21
$\frac{3}{4}$ bushel (24 quarts)	3 plant group	6	32	36
per plant				
Hardy, Group VII	1 plant	9	17	19
Tropical without	3 plant group	9	29	32
manure/fertiliser.	1 plant	6	21	24
1 bushel per plant	3 plant group	6	36	41

*Figures for container depth allow for a $\frac{1}{2}$-inch to 1-inch finishing layer of gravel or small pebbles over the soil.

least a 50 per cent mixture of lighter soil or rotted turf with it (or even peat at a pinch) if roots are to develop well. Except for this purpose, peat has no value in the pond. Leafmould and garden compost will foul the water and must never be used.

The use of manure and fertiliser poses problems. If optimum plant growth is the only consideration, use them. Remember, however, that they will enrich the water with nutrients and promote the growth of algae as well as lilies. There is a strong case for their use with tropical lilies which have a lot of growing to do in a short season and need plenty of nourishment to maintain a high level of flower production. Traditionally each plant is reckoned to need a bushel (32 quarts) of soil, though some professional growers consider two-thirds of that to be adequate. The difference, perhaps, is between plain soil and soil boosted with manure and fertiliser. A bushel of good garden loam, especially if mixed with chopped or rotted turf (sod), will do perfectly well. If a richer mixture is created by using one part of rotted cow manure to three or four parts of soil, with the addition of half a pound of fine bonemeal, then three-quarters of a bushel will suffice for one season's growth. Special water lily fertiliser offered by nurseries can be substituted for the bone meal, used at the rate they recommend. Bonemeal, in my view, is of doubtful effectiveness and prone to sour the water as it decomposes. The richer mixture can be used for hardy lilies too if plant growth is the primary interest. Most water gardeners, not wishing to increase the risk of algal bloom, use a heavy loam/turf mixture and get very satisfactory results.

Since waterlilies vary enormously in vigour it follows that the amount of soil needed to sustain their growth must vary too. The 'one bushel per plant' idea cannot be true for all of them. If a bushel is needed for a vigorous lily, a miniature lily will clearly get by on much less. Or, to look at it another way, a bushel will feed a dwarf lily for much longer than it will a vigorous one. The list of container sizes on p. 57 is an attempt to define acceptable container sizes to provide an adequate volume of soil for lilies in different categories of vigour. For tropical lilies it is enough for one season, assuming annual replacement of plants and soil. The volumes allowed for hardy lilies should be adequate for three years. None will object if given a larger container, with a longer interval between soil changes. They can be grown in a smaller volume of soil if it is replaced more frequently.

Since a quicker and bolder effect can be achieved, particularly in large ponds, by planting three lilies of one variety as a group, container sizes are given for single plants and three-plant groups in each category. Alternative shapes, i.e. square or circular, are given, with two alternative depths; the dimensions of any boxes or bowls you have handy can be checked against these to determine their usefulness. Of the two alternative shapes given in each case the shallower is to be preferred. For example the 8 quarts required for a single lily in Group III will be provided by a container 8 inches square and 9 inches deep, or by one 11 inches square and 6 inches deep; the wider, shallower alternative is the best.

It so happens that the quarter bushel container of this example is the size of a square plastic container with perforated sides widely offered to British water gardeners as a 'lily basket'. For small and medium-sized lilies it is excellent, with a soil change every three years. For Group IV and Group V lilies it will do if the soil is changed every other year. Used for Group VI lilies the soil will need changing annually. Group VII types are altogether too big for it.

Perforated sides, incidentally, have some value in a deep container with a small surface area in improving the exchange of dissolved gases between soil and water. In wide shallow containers this is achieved by the large surface area of soil in contact with water and perforated sides are unnecessary.

Planting Tropical Lilies

Using a heavy loam/turf mixture, a container with internal dimensions 21 inches square and 6 inches deep will hold a bushel of soil covered with an inch of gravel. A container 18 inches square and 6 inches deep will be big enough if the soil mix includes manure and fertiliser. The 2-foot square by 1-foot deep container sometimes recommended (volume 3 bushels!) is unnecessarily wasteful.

Tropical lily roots are planted upright, with the crown clear of soil, preferably straight into a container already in the pond, and not before the water temperature is holding close to 70°F (21°C). Tropical leaves are thin and wither quickly if exposed to the sun out of water. The plants will settle faster and bloom sooner if they have only 4 inches of water over the container for the first month. They can then be lowered to 6 or, at the very most, 8 inches. Once tropicals are planted, any chilling of the water must be avoided at all costs and a major water change is out of the question. That must be completed at least a week before planting time. After planting, topping up to make good evaporation loss must be done slowly on a little-and-often basis.

Planting Hardy Lilies

The roots of hardy lilies are either long fleshy rhizomes or roughly pyramidal chunks with a growing point at the apex and a tangle of root below. Broken or lengthy roots are cut off and any mature leaves removed. They will only die back anyway. If the supplier has already done this, leaving only short new leaf shoots, do not be alarmed, they are all that is needed. You probably will not have the heart to remove any half-opened flower buds but do not be surprised when they come to nothing. Do not – if you make a choice in a garden centre – pick a plant just because it has a flower. Pick a good rootstock; when it has settled in the flowers will come.

Plant the long rhizome type of rootstock almost horizontally, about an inch below the soil surface, just tilted to bring the growing tip above the surface. Firm the soil, place a flat stone over the buried root so that there is no risk of it coming adrift, cover the remaining soil surface with gravel (sand is too easily disturbed by fish) and make sure the growing tip is not buried. The chunky rootstock (as in the *marliacea* varieties) are planted upright, again ensuring that the growing point is not buried. Submerge the container gently, until 8–10 inches of water cover it, propping it up if necessary on bricks (but not on cement blocks). After a week or two, leaves and stems should have developed sufficiently for the container to be finally settled at the depth appropriate to the variety in it.

Planting Oxygenators
Since the roots of oxygenators are for anchorage rather than feeding they need not be planted in soil. A rooting medium that will not muddy the water has obvious advantages and they will grow happily in gravel. Anything from pinhead-sized aquarium sand to $\frac{1}{8}$-inch pea shingle will do very well and it need only be an inch or two deep. A 14-inch by 8-inch plastic seed tray is ideal for 5 or 6 bunches, and almost any sort of shallow container can be pressed into service for this purpose.

When large numbers of oxygenators are required it becomes inconvenient to have dozens of small containers scattered about the pond; a few large planting areas would be better. The simplest solution I have found so far involves the use of the 4-inch wide plastic or aluminium strip sold in garden centres for edging lawns. A length of either of these materials, the ends joined with pop rivets to make a circle, is placed on the pool floor and half filled with gravel. I find that this can be done quite successfully even in a filled pond. The plastic strip tries to float, but only needs three stones leaned on it to keep it in place until the gravel is put in. These 'containers' cannot be moved or lifted out, of course, but in view of the weight of gravel in them it would hardly be possible anyway.

1. Albatross

2. Odalisque

3. Newton

4. Laydekerhoucle

5. Amabilis

6. Comanche

7. Candida

8. Mrs Richmond

9. Peter D. Slocum (Lotus)

10. Daubeniana (tropical)

11. Mrs George C. Hitchcock (night-blooming tropical)

12. *N. marliacea albida*

13. *N. marliacea carnea*

14. *N. marliacea chromatella*

15. James Brydon

16. Sunrise

17. Mme. Wilfron Gonnère

18. Attraction (young plant)

19. Attraction (mature plant)

20. Gloriosa

21. *N. laydekeri fulgens*

22. *N. laydekeri lilacea*

23. *N. laydekeri purpurata*

24. Froebeli

25. Gonnère

26. Paul Hariot

27. Graziella

28. Conqueror

29. Lucida

30. Masaniello

31. Rose Arey

32. Rene Gerard

33. Helen Fowler

34. Charles de Meurville

35. Wm. Falconer

36. *N. atropurpurea* with yellow Comet Goldfish, uncoloured goldfish and Koi Carp

37. Gladstoniana

38. *Caltha palustris plena*

39. *Caltha palustris*

40. *Eriophorum*

41. *Pontederia cordata*

42. *Iris laevigata* and *Iris laevigata alba*

43. *Iris laevigata colchesteri*

44. *Nymphoides peltata*

45. *Aponogeton distachyus*

46. *Lobelia cardinalis*

47. *Sagittaria sagittifolia*

48. Iris Rose Queen

49. *Eichhornia*

50. *Osmunda regalis*

51. *Gunnera manicata*

52. *Primula helodoxa*

53. *Rodgersia*

54. *Iris kaempferi*

55. *Hosta crispula*

56. *Cistus lusitanicus decumbens*

57. *Geranium subcaulescens splendens*

58. Formal pond in a walled garden

59. An indoor water feature needs abundant light

60. A place to soothe the mind and refresh the spirit

61. The pond in winter, showing how to prevent ice covering the entire surface

62. A waterfall enhances the natural surrounds of the pond

63. Simple, formal, lines here perfectly match the setting

64. Marginal plants and shrubs make a backcloth for tranquil water

A strip $9\frac{1}{2}$ feet long joined to make a circle 3 feet in diameter needs 1 hundredweight of $\frac{1}{8}$-inch gravel for a depth of 2 inches; it would take 40 oxygenators planted 5 inches apart or 30 planted 6 inches apart. A $12\frac{1}{2}$-foot strip making a circle 4 feet in diameter needs 200 lb of gravel and takes 70 plants 5 inches apart or 50 plants 6 inches apart. A 15-foot strip makes a circle large enough to take 100 plants 5 inches apart, 70 plants 6 inches apart, and needs $2\frac{1}{2}$ hundredweight of gravel.

Oxygenators are usually supplied as unrooted cuttings, with a twist of lead holding several stems in a bunch. It is optimistic to drop these in and expect them to stay put until roots develop. They barely have negative buoyancy and will just drift till a few bits root and most break up. To root them quickly each bunch needs to be pushed well into the soil or gravel, made firm, and allowed to grow without interference from fish. In large planting areas a speedier method is to lay the bunches flat on the gravel, then stretch small-mesh plastic netting tightly over them, anchoring it with stones. This way I find that growth is slow to start but once started is rapid and very dense. *Ceratophyllum* (Hornwort) is the exception that you can 'just drop in'.

Planting Marginals

The worst mistake commonly made in planting marginals is to mix varieties in the same pocket or container. This can only mean unequal competition and the most vigorous ultimately chokes the rest. Marginal troughs, as are sometimes incorporated in concrete ponds, should be subdivided with barriers of brick or stone, leaving a clear gap without soil between each planted section. Each section may have several plants, but they will be of the same variety. Straying roots will find nothing to encourage them and can easily be spotted and dealt with. The same applies to individual containers standing on the marginal shelf of a liner pond. Something 9 to 12 inches across and 5 or 6 inches deep will take 2 or 3 plants of most marginal types, for the sake of quick effect. One container, one variety, means bold clumps with greater ornamental effect. From 2 to 4 inches of water over the container will suit most marginals. Fine adjustments to cater for special cases (Iris Rose Queen, for example) are easily made by raising the container on a tile or two.

Planting floating plants is a contradiction in terms and barely merits a paragraph. Just drop them in. Do not be surprised if *Stratiotes* or *Lemna trisulca* fail to float; they will when the mood takes them.

109

The best advice that can be given about planting in general is to have soil, containers, gravel (and muscular help if large containers will have to be moved) organised in advance, and to complete the job with all possible speed. Plants awaiting attention should be immersed in water unless in moisture-retaining wrappings. Planting should not be done out in the sun. Oxygenators dry out and shrivel up in no time and must not be kept out of the water a moment longer than necessary. Hardy lilies, if not moved into the pond immediately they are planted, must be stood in the shade, covered with wet newspaper, and moved into the pond as soon as all are ready.

Tropical Water Lilies

It might fairly be claimed that the tropical water lilies out-perform the hardy lilies in every department (except, of course, the not unimportant matter of winter hardiness in non-tropical regions).

Certainly the tropicals have, in the main, larger leaves and a greater spread; they have more flowers, larger flowers and, in most cases, more fragrant flowers. Their rainbow spectrum of colours includes blue, purple, violet, lavender and even greenish shades that do not occur at all among the hardies. Flowers 10 inches in diameter are commonplace, and some varieties regularly achieve more than 12 inches. They are raised anything from 6 to 18 inches above the surface. The tropicals include both day-blooming and night-blooming varieties which between them offer 24 hours of bloom in every day.

Tropicals are at risk in temperatures below 65°F (18°C) but they will flourish outdoors in temperate regions if the plants are not put out until night temperatures are consistently warm. In those regions where summer temperatures are erratic, cultivation in an unheated greenhouse reduces risk, improves flowering performance and extends the flowering season. Tropicals are often still blooming well when the hardies are in decline, but when water temperatures eventually drop they become dormant. The bulbs can be stored in damp sand but some expertise is required to overwinter tropical bulbs successfully; the majority of gardeners treat tropical lilies as annuals and replace them every year.

Most tropicals have very large leaves, often with scalloped or crimped edges. Often speckled, splashed or boldly patterned with chestnut or purple, the leaves of some varieties are almost as beautiful as the flowers.

Day-blooming tropicals

The flowers of day-blooming tropical lilies open in the forenoon and close at dusk.

Some varieties have the intriguing habit of producing tiny plantlets in the middle of mature leaves. These miniatures, complete with tiny leaves, a bulb and roots, can be detached from the parent leaf and potted to produce new plants. Such varieties are known as viviparous forms, and, since some produce plantlets more freely than others, they have been marked in the descriptive list that follows either as V, for viviparous, or as VV for very viviparous.

The viviparous lilies are the hardiest of the tropicals and will stand lower temperatures early and late in the season without going dormant. In areas such as Britain where summer temperatures are notoriously inconsistent, viviparous varieties are the best choice since they will have a better chance of surviving occasional cool spells.

The work of hybridisers, mainly American, has produced an astonishing range of hues and colours. With almost every water lily nursery having its own novelties, the available hybrids are far too numerous to be completely listed here. The varieties described have in the main been selected as being the best liked and the most widely available.

The varietal name is followed (where appropriate) by the plate number in brackets, and by the name of the raiser.

Afterglow. MARTIN RANDIG.
Yellow centre, suffused with pink and shading to burnished orange in the outer petal. Growth adaptable to small pools.

Alice Tricker. WILLIAM TRICKER.
Well shaped flowers of substance with broad white petals. A strong grower that flowers generously.

American Beauty. GEORGE PRING.
A deep rose pink that is almost red. Flowers averaging 8 inches in diameter are regarded as 'moderate' by tropical standards.

Aviator Pring. GEORGE PRING.
Very large, deep yellow, cup-shaped blooms raised high above the water. An exceptionally free-flowering variety. The green leaves have crimped edges.

Bagdad. GEORGE PRING.
Wide, flat flowers, wisteria blue with gold centres, are carried just above richly mottled leaves.

Blue Beauty. WILLIAM TRICKER.
A long-standing favourite with lilac to deep blue flowers 10 to 12

inches in diameter. Free blooming and very fragrant, it will adjust quite happily to life in a tub.

Bob Trickett. GEORGE PRING.
Yellow centred campanula-blue flowers that can be as much as 14 inches across. The green leaves have red undersides with green veining.

Colorata. African species.
Listed sometimes as Blue Pygmy, this charming lily is the ideal subject for tub culture. The 3–4-inch flowers have violet petals paler at the base, and purple stamens. Very fragrant and prolific.

Daubeniana (10). DR. DAUBENY. VV.
Lavender blue flowers 2–3 inches across, very fragrant and abundant. A real miniature, ideal for indoor pools and tubs. It needs less sun than most.

Director George T. Moore. GEORGE PRING.
Glowing rich purple-blue flowers 8–10 inches across, with purple stamens and a yellow centre. Blooms freely. Compact leaf growth.

Enchantment. MARTIN RANDIG.
Deep salmon rose blooms with elegant narrow petals. A coronet of pink stamens encircles the orange yellow centre. The flowers are large and abundant.

Evelyn Randig. MARTIN RANDIG.
Very large, deep pink flowers freely produced. Leaves spotted and striped with chestnut and purple.

General Pershing. GEORGE PRING.
Possibly the greatest favourite of all, for several good reasons. The 8–10-inch blooms, bright pink with pink-tipped yellow stamens, are very double, very fragrant, and open up to 12 hours a day. It is certainly the finest of the orchid-pink varieties.

Golden West. MARTIN RANDIG.
Flowers open a delicate salmon pink and mature to apricot with a golden centre. They are fragrant and held high above the mottled leaves.

Green Smoke. MARTIN RANDIG.
From the golden centre delicate shades of yellow and chartreuse green flow into smoky blue at the petal tip. This beautiful and unique blend of subtle colours crowns fifteen years of patient work by the raiser.

Isabelle Pring. GEORGE PRING. VV.
Crisp pure white fragrant blooms up to 10 inches in diameter: stamens golden yellow. Relatively compact leaf growth.

Jack Wood. JOHN WOOD.
Large fragrant and strikingly beautiful blooms for whose rich colour 'raspberry red' is a most inadequate description. The leaves are lightly splashed with purple.

Margaret Randig. MARTIN RANDIG. V.
One of the largest, with fully opening broad-petalled sky blue flowers with yellow centres. Blooms very generously. Heavily mottled foliage.

Midnight. GEORGE PRING.
Dusky crimson-purple blooms 6–7 inches across. Though not as large as some, the flowers are double, deliciously fragrant and abundant.

Mrs C.W. Ward. WILLIAM TRICKER.
Bright rose pink 8–10-inch flowers often held more than 12 inches above the surface. The golden stamens are tipped with pink.

Mrs Martin E. Randig. MARTIN RANDIG. V.
Splendid blooms with a rich heady fragrance, maturing from mauve-blue to deep blue-purple. Leaves green with a bronzy underside.

Pamela. AUGUST KOCH.
Really true blue flowers 10 to 12 inches in diameter are produced very freely and held high above the chestnut-marbled leaves.

Panama Pacific. WILLIAM TRICKER. V.
One of the classic tropicals, with rich wine-red blooms that deepen to plum-purple: yellow stamens are tipped with purple. Strong and free-flowering.

Patricia Pat. WILLIAM TRICKER. V.
Usually listed simply as Patricia, this is a small grower, very suitable for tubs, with a profusion of crimson blooms.

Peach Blow. GEORGE PRING. VV.
Full, many-petalled flowers, pink with a peach centre. The golden stamens are pink-tipped.

Persian Lilac. GEORGE PRING.
Solid lilac-pink blooms well filled with broad petals; golden stamens tipped with pink. An outstanding variety with relatively small bright green leaves.

Pink Platter. GEORGE PRING. V.
Flat-opening blooms with long tapering clear pink petals: pink-tipped golden stamens.

Royal Purple. BUSKIRK. V.
Glowing purple flowers 6–8 inches in diameter. A moderate grower that does well in tubs.

St Louis. GEORGE PRING.
The first yellow tropical hybrid lily, the first water lily patented in the United States, and a great favourite. The light yellow stellate flowers average 10 inches in diameter.

St Louis Gold. GEORGE PRING.
A consistently good performer, ideal for small pools and tubs. Deep yellow flowers 7–8 inches across are produced with great freedom.

Talisman. GEORGE PRING. VV.
Opens pale yellow flushed with pink. As the bloom matures the pink spreads and the yellow deepens, producing a beautiful combination of colours.

Yellow Dazzler. MARTIN RANDIG.
A very free-flowering hybrid with flat-opening double blooms of rich chrome yellow.

Night-blooming tropicals
The night-blooming tropical lilies include some of the largest and most dramatically beautiful of all flowers. They are particularly enjoyed by those members of the family who are not at home before the day-blooming varieties, hardy or tropical, have closed up. The flowers of the night-bloomers open at dusk and remain open until the sun is high on the following day, perhaps until noon. When it is cloudy and cool they may stay open all day. It is in the evening, however, that their exotic beauty, illuminated by moonlight or floodlight, and their delicate fragrance, are most appreciated.

 Though the flowers dislike the heat of the sun, the plants do not, and for maximum growth and flowering performance it is essential for the night-blooming tropicals to be planted where they will get all the sunshine possible. It will help, too, if their roots, even after a month with 4 inches of water over them, are never covered by more than 6 inches. Five feet between plants is close enough.

Emily Grant Hutchings. GEORGE PRING.
An exceptionally free bloomer with deep pink flowers that seems to be everybody's favourite. The centre of each long curved petal is slightly paler than the rest, giving the bloom remarkable definition and brightness.

H.C. Haarstick. JAMES GURNEY.
Dramatically vivid red blooms 10 to 12 inches in diameter. A strong grower and a wonderfully consistent performer.

Maroon Beauty. PERRY SLOCUM.
A handsome new variety with deep maroon blooms, in shade somewhere between H.C. Haarstick and Red Flare. The flowers are frequently 12 inches in diameter.

Missouri. GEORGE PRING.
Magnificent broad-petalled creamy white flowers, often 13 inches across, that show up particularly well at night. Coppery brown young leaves mature to dark green.

Mrs George C. Hitchcock (11). GEORGE PRING.
Rich orchid pink flowers that have been known to exceed 14 inches in diameter. A reliable grower and a very free bloomer.

Mrs John A. Wood. JOHN WOOD.
A fine new maroon red lily; not unlike Red Flare, but the red is not quite as dark and the blooms are larger.

Red Flare. MARTIN RANDIG.
The deepest dusky red blooms and the richest foliage of any water lily. The leaves are deep mahogany red.

Sir Galahad. MARTIN RANDIG.
Large pure white flowers with yellow stamens. A crisper white and more abundant bloomer than Missouri.

Lotus (Nelumbium)

The sacred Lotus of the ancients, together with American and Asiatic species and the hybrids derived from them, form a group of very beautiful and impressive aquatic plants. Their blue-green leaves, often 2 feet across, are raised above the water as high as 4 to 8 feet and little will grow under their dense shade. Their roots demand a lot of room. For these reasons they are often given the freedom of a pond to themselves, behind the main pond, where they make a very impressive and beautiful backcloth.

Lotus flowers, displayed clear of the leaves, may be as much as 10 to 12 inches across, with a spicy fragrance. Each falls after about 4 days and leaves a massive seed pod much prized, when dried, by flower arrangers.

Nelumbium speciosum is pink; *N. luteum*, yellow; *N. album*, white; *N. flavescens*, cream; *N. roseum plenum*, deep rose pink and double. Among the hybrids **Peter D. Slocum (9)**, starting pink, becoming yellow and finally cream, is outstanding. The dwarf hybrid **Momo Botan**, with 2 to 3-inch pink flowers, is a charming rarity.

Lotus need a rich soil and at least a bushel of it per plant. A mixture of 7 parts soil (a quarter of which should be clay if possible) to 1 of fertiliser or rotted cow manure is recommended. A container about 3 feet across and 12 inches deep is desirable; plants grow better in round than in square containers. Half-barrels are suitable. The tuber, like an elongated banana, should be handled with care as the one or two growing points are brittle and damage can destroy the plant's chances. In planting, the tuber is slanted so that the thick end is 2 inches deep, and the sharp growing point extends $\frac{1}{4}$ to $\frac{1}{2}$-inch clear of soil. This is vital to success. Place a flat rock over the tuber, but not on the point. Have only 2–4 inches of water at first, later increasing this to 6–8 inches.

Lotus are hardy enough to winter successfully outdoors wherever they get plenty of hot summer sunshine to thoroughly ripen the tubers. This includes most of the United States and Continental Europe, but not Britain.

116

5
Livestock

It is usual to recommend an interval between planting a new pond and introducing fish. This is for the sake of the oxygenating plants which can be destroyed if not given time to root and get well established before fish begin foraging among them. However, if oxygenators are protected by a rough dome of crumpled small mesh wire netting, can fish not be installed immediately? They can, assuming that a week has elapsed since the pond was filled, ensuring the dispersal of chlorine and the achievement of ambient temperature. It would still, in my view, however, be desirable to wait a month. In that time the natural development of innumerable invisible organisms will modify the chemistry of the water, maturing it in many subtle ways to a much more comfortable environment for fish than the raw tap water you started with. Whether it is hard or soft, alkaline or acid, will not greatly worry the sort of fish that are likely to occupy it unless it runs to quite exceptional extremes. In any case you have to use the water supply you have, and there is not much you can or need to do to change it. Nature's alchemy, operating through the growth and decay of plant life, and the living processes of fish and other organisms, works steadily to modify any extremes you may start with.

A month after the pond has been planted it is more than likely that the water will be decidedly coloured; it may even be as thick as pea soup. Do not imagine for a moment that you will be doing the fish a favour by changing it. They will like it, however unappetising it may look to you, far better than raw new water.

As to numbers, you can please yourself, up to a point. That point depends on the surface area of the pond and not, as is sometimes suggested, on the gallonage. A pond 6 feet deep will support no more fish than if it was 2 feet deep. The pond surface, the lung through which it breathes in oxygen and exhales carbon dioxide, is the limiting factor. The limit is sometimes expressed as so many inches of fish for each square foot of surface area. This implies that a pond could have, say, either 10 6-inch fish or 30 2-inch fish, since either way it adds up to 60 fish-inches. Small fish grow, however, and soon

The Golden Orfe, lively and colourful, is always active in pursuit of mosquitos, midges and other insect nuisances.

make nonsense of such calculations. The only safe way to avoid the consequences of eventual overcrowding is to work on the likely mature size of the fish, regardless of how big they are when first introduced. On this basis (and I am talking now about fish other than Koi, Higoi and common carp) I believe the maximum is one fish for every 2 square feet. I also believe in not stocking up to the limit. One fish for every 3 square feet of surface area, regardless of size, is as many as I would care to recommend if there is to be room for healthy growth, for breeding, and for a safety margin during those spells of thundery weather when, for short periods, the pond can become critically overloaded with carbon dioxide. If you are tempted to try Koi or Higoi carp in a pond without a sophisticated filtration system you would be wise to allow at least 25 square feet of surface area for each one.

I emphasise that you do not need to stock up to the limit. Fish are not compulsory, and a pond can be perfectly successful without them – but it will certainly be the poorer in terms of liveliness, colour and interest. A few at least are recommended for a purely practical reason. Mosquitos, gnats and midges spend part of their life cycle in water and will regard your pond as an invitation to breed. A few fish will completely prevent any such nuisance.

Goldfish have long been the most popular pond fish because they are hardy, colourful and relatively inexpensive. They are usually red or orange, sometimes yellow or white, and on occasion combine these colours with black or silver markings. Centuries of selective breeding have produced many variations in colour and shape, only a few of which are suitable for outdoor ponds.

Shubunkins are essentially goldfish whose scales are not shiny and whose colour is a mottled mixture of red, blue, brown, black and white. So-called Blue Shubunkins are not entirely blue: they just have a higher proportion of blue-grey colouring than ordinary shubunkins. Comets have extra long tails and fins: there are Comet Goldfish and Comet Shubunkins. Fantails have short deep rounded bodies and flowing double tails. Fantail Goldfish are typically red and shiny; Calico Fantails have the mottled shubunkin coloration. The goggle-eyed black Moor is a poor pondfish, on the score of visibility if

*A Giant Ramshorn Snail (*Planorbis corneus*). Although they do much less damage than* Limnaea, *even Ramshorns cannot resist the leaves of Frog-bit (twice natural size).*

nothing else. Visibility, after all, is a prime consideration, and here a good red goldfish or comet takes some beating. The mottled colour mixture of some varieties, beautiful when seen in an aquarium, acts more like a camouflage pattern against a pond background. All these goldfish varieties, being derived from one species, are capable of interbreeding. A pond stocked initially with goldfish, comets and fantails will in the fullness of time contain a mongrel mixture that regresses steadily towards the basic shape unless the owner ruthlessly weeds out the rogues to maintain the comet and longtail strains. The common ancestry of all goldfish varieties gives them an over-all similarity. Their natural inclination to grub about on the bottom, their movement patterns, their temperament and their whole character are much of a muchness. It makes a refreshing contrast to introduce into the pond a fish which is not only colourful but totally different from the goldfish tribe in movement and character. The Golden Orfe is a slender lively fish, bright salmon gold in colour; it is sudden death to any insect that so much as touches the surface and it is nearly always visible. It should never be put into very small ponds (it will jump out) but in every other respect it is a superb pondfish.

There are other fish that can be kept in garden ponds but they do not compare with those already mentioned. Tench are often credited with the ability to 'doctor' sick fish but there is absolutely no evidence for it. They are alleged to 'keep the bottom clean' as if they could be expected to go over the bottom like aquatic vacuum cleaners sucking up dirt. Certainly they are bottom feeders ready to forage for food fragments in the mud but all they do to the dirt is stir it up. As scavengers goldfish are just as effective and a good deal more visible. Catfish, sometimes recommended as scavengers, are a menace that should never be deliberately introduced into a garden pond. Other predators such as pike, perch and bass have no place there either.

Introduction of Fish to the Pond

When fish are introduced into the pond – and on any other occasion when fish are transferred from one body of water to another – the greatest care must be taken to avoid a sharp temperature change. They can tolerate a very wide range of temperatures and cope with natural fluctuations that always happen gradually. Nevertheless, being poured from a bag into water 20 degrees cooler produces, in a creature whose body temperature is that of its surroundings, a traumatic shock that makes it fatally vulnerable to disease. That is why changes of pond water, with fish being thoughtlessly moved from pond water to cold chlorinated tap water, are followed so

120

*A Great Pond Snail (*Limnaea stagnalis*) (× $1\frac{1}{2}$) carrying on its shell an egg rope laid by another* Limnaea. *Plant stems and the undersides of lily leaves are more usual sites for the sausage-shaped egg capsules (below).*

frequently by fungus infection. All that is necessary to avoid trouble is to float the travelling bag, or the temporary container, in the pond for an hour to cause a gradual equalisation of temperature before the fish are turned loose.

Quarantine

Reputable fish dealers go to a good deal of trouble to maintain disease-free stocks. Even so, it is very desirable that new purchases should be quarantined for a time just in case one of them is incubating an ailment. This is particularly important if newcomers are to be introduced into a pond already holding a stock of healthy, highly-prized fish.

An aerated aquarium will do for a few small fish, but not for larger specimens, or Orfe. Uncramped outdoor quarters are better, and this is one of several situations which emphasise the value of a second pond. After a course of Sterazin (unless Orfe are present) or similar treatment to deal with any flukes, anchor worm and fish lice, follow up 10 days later with a dose of Myxazin or other anti-bacterial medication. Then, after a further 7-day wait-and-see period, fish showing no signs of ill health can be transferred to the main pond.

Many other uses will be found for the second pond. When adult fish are 'driving' they can be transferred to spawn in it, and then be returned promptly to the main pond. Alternatively, plants loaded with spawn dropped in the main pond can be transferred to what now becomes a nursery where fry can hatch and grow free from the danger of adult fish. Plants can be raised there too; cuttings of oxygenators and water lily offsets, so vulnerable to the attentions of adult fish, can be grown into strong plants well rooted in containers before transfer to the main pond. When no fish are present the second pond, stocked with *Daphnia*, becomes a reservoir of fish food as well as plant stock. And when it is necessary to clear out the main pond one of the trickiest problems – what to do with the fish – will have been solved in advance.

Quite understandably, few gardeners contemplating pond construction think initially in terms of more than one pond. Later, with the confidence born of experience, many embark on a second, larger pond. This becomes the main feature and the first becomes the reserve. The mistake often made at this point is in trying to link the two by means of a waterfall or a connecting channel. In fact there is nothing to be gained by joining them. All the benefits of the reserve/quarantine/hospital/fry-rearing/plant-raising/food reservoir pond depend upon the two bodies of water being unconnected.

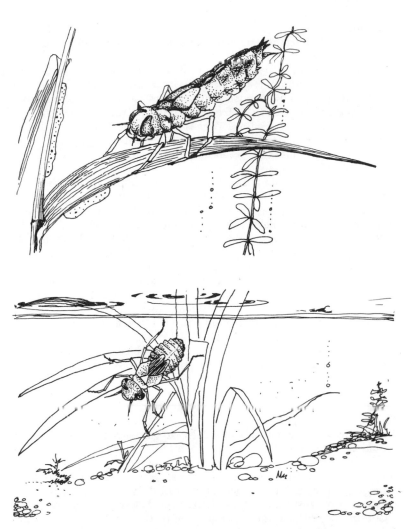

There are many species of dragonflies, varying considerably in size and colouring. The underwater larval stages, known as nymphs, two examples of which are shown here, also vary greatly in size and body shape. They may spend three or four years as stealthy hunters of other aquatic creatures (including small fish and other dragonfly nymphs) before emerging as adult dragonflies.

Feeding

Give the fish two or three days to settle down before feeding them. In a new pool feeding will be necessary; in a mature well-planted one fish will find much of what they need. It still pays, though, to feed them up in the autumn, ready for the winter fast, and in the spring to help them get over it. Novice pond-owners worry a lot about how much food and how often to feed it, having been led to believe that fish are killed by overfeeding. That is not true, in that they will not gorge themselves to death. It is true to the extent that excess uneaten food will decay, pollute the water and create unhygienic conditions in which fish easily contract disease.

To the question of how much there is no simple answer, because appetite depends on activity, and activity depends on water temperature; and water temperature varies considerably. When temperature drops appetite drops. Below 40°F (4.5°C) it fades and when it is really cold the fish metabolism slows right down and food cannot be digested. So the only rule has to be: feed when the fish are active and obviously interested and give them, once a day, as much as they will clear up in five minutes. Make a habit of tapping the pool surround sharply immediately before putting food on the water. It is surprising how quickly the fish put two and two together and react to the signal. When they do not respond they do not need food and none should be left.

What sort of food? Ants 'eggs' and the crumb type of fishfood have very little value, but there are many good fishfoods available in pellet or flake form. Keep several and ring the changes; good health requires a varied diet.

Snails

I have always had doubts about snails. No gardener in his right mind would collect snails, let alone buy them, in order to turn them loose among his lettuces. Why do it to the pond? The reason usually offered is that snails keep the pond clear. Since they have no effect whatever on the colour of the water I can only suppose this to be a corruption by wishful thinkers of the idea that snails keep the pond clean. In that, at least, there is a grain of truth. Snails will eat surplus fishfood, drowned worms, fish wastes and algae; but they produce wastes too, and their effect on algae always seems pitifully inadequate. They may feed on decaying plant remains but some feed even more readily on healthy plant tissues. On the whole I am inclined to believe that you are just as well off without them. *Planorbis corneus*, the large Ramshorn, and various small species that

A brand new dragonfly clings to the empty nymphal case from which it has just emerged. It may be be many hours before the wings are fully expanded and flight is possible (× 1½).

come in on new plants, can be tolerated. The one that British water gardeners need to beware of is *Limnaea stagnalis*. He has a conical pointed shell up to 2 inches long and a great appetite for plants. His egg capsules, sausage-shaped blobs of clear jelly, should be carefully removed from the stems and leaves of any new plants. The snail itself can be attracted by bait in the form of grapefruit rinds and crushed lettuce leaves floated on the water overnight.

If I am in two minds about snails, I have no doubts on the subject of mussels in a garden pond. They are not a good idea (see p. 142).

Visitors

Apart from livestock deliberately introduced the pond will be adopted by a number of eager colonisers, nature's fascinating free gift for anyone who takes the trouble to make a water garden. All of them are interesting and most of them can be welcomed but the water gardener needs to know how to recognise and deal with the few exceptions.

Some of the airborne arrivals have already been mentioned. Mosquitos and similar nuisances will try to use the pond as a breeding place. The presence of a few goldfish or Golden Orfe will ensure that they are completely unsuccessful. Dragonflies and slender

125

The Great Diving Beetle, Dytiscus marginalis, *well over an inch long, is capable of killing fish much larger than itself. The need to breathe air periodically at the surface makes it vulnerable to netting.*

Damselflies may be more successful. Some of the eggs they deposit will hatch into nymphs that will lurk in thick underwater vegetation for up to four years, depending on species. The emergence of a dragonfly from the ugly nymph that has crawled up a reed stem is a marvellous thing to watch. In the air the dragonfly gets full marks as an incredible flying machine and as a snapper-up of insects. In its underwater existence the nymph gets a black mark for including fish fry among the victims it stalks among the oxygenator stems.

There will be a profusion of beetles ranging in size from rice-grain up to nearly 2 inches. It is worth remembering that small beetles do not grow into large beetles. When it emerges from the pupa as an adult beetle it is as large as it is ever going to be. This means you can safely ignore all the little ones and just concentrate on the big predatory types. The most dangerous fish predator in both Britain and North America is the Great Diving Beetle. The adult beetle, up to $1\frac{1}{2}$ inches long and $\frac{3}{4}$ inch across the back, is blackish with a narrow edge of brownish gold. The larva has a light brown tapering curved body up to 2 inches long. The bristles in its tail are breathing tubes, not a sting. Both larva and beetle are ferocious killers of any soft-bodied pond dwellers, including fish. They suck the juices out of their prey; fish corpses that appear undamaged except for small puncture wounds are usually victims of the Diving Beetle. Since both the larva and the adult beetle have to surface periodically to take in a fresh supply of air, they are not difficult to spot and net out.

Water Boatmen need the same treatment. Only about $\frac{1}{2}$-inch long, they are recognisable as the ones that swim, and rest at the surface, upside-down. The name comes from the extra-long hind legs which work like oars. Water Boatmen kill small fish and fry.

Not all pond beetles are aquatic. The Water Lily Beetle, an inconspicuous brown creature smaller than a ladybird, lives on the top of lily pads where, in company with its dark grey grubs, it cuts wandering channels in the leaf tissue. Heavily attacked leaves decay into a black spongy mess. Normally fish cannot reach the pest but if the foliage can be submerged for a few days, either by the weight of metal mesh or by raising the water level, the insects should soon be polished off. Fortunately this pest is only common where lilies are grown in quantity and it seldom turns up in small garden ponds. It is as well to examine the leaves of newly acquired lilies before planting to make sure they carry no beetles, grubs or tiny yellow egg clusters.

The underside of the leaf will bear close examination too. Apart from the egg clusters of snails already described it may have embedded in it the small leathery dark brown egg capsules of leeches. Most

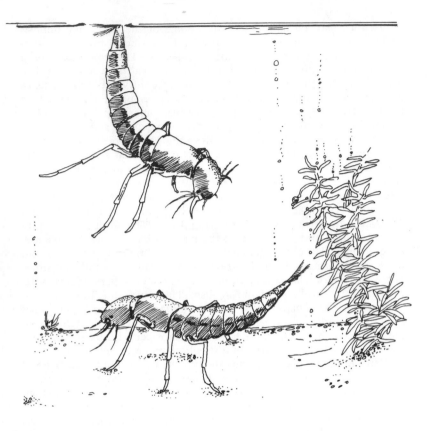

The larval form of Dytiscus *is as ferocious a predator as the adult beetle. Even as it hangs at the surface taking in air through tail appendages, its jaws are spread ready to seize prey.*

of these unattractive creatures feed on snails and other slow soft-bodied creatures but if there is a shortage of this sort of prey they may turn to fish.

Oval holes about an inch long in a lily leaf show where the caterpillar of a China Marks Moth has been busy. Depending on the species, the caterpillar may live snugly between a cut-out piece and the underside of the leaf, the two being firmly joined with silk: or he may walk around the pond wearing two joined pieces like sandwich boards. The damage done to the leaf is not serious enough to trouble the lilies.

Amphibians

Frogs, toads, and newts spend most of their time out of water living such unobtrusive lives that we are seldom aware of them. It is only when they turn up in the pond in the spring to deposit eggs that they are really noticed: and are assumed incorrectly to be mainly aquatic creatures. Their mobility makes them independent. Whether they will adopt your pond or not is their choice. If you introduce them and they do not care for it they will depart and there is no way you can stop them. If conditions are favourable they will simply arrive and nothing you can do will keep them out. What cannot be cured must be endured: but are they really something the water gardener need worry about? If he is dedicated to rearing fish fry to maturity in the greatest possible numbers he certainly needs to worry about newts (salamanders in North America). They will eat small wriggling creatures of any kind, whether they are worms or midge larvae or fish fry, so the devoted fish breeder must net them out. They represent no danger to adult fish.

The same cannot be said with absolute certainty about the frog. Frogs in the grip of spring fever will eagerly grab at anything that moves in the hope, presumably, that it will turn out to be a female frog. Try moving your finger, or a stick, in the water near one if you do not believe this. Operating on this trial and error, if-it-moves-grab-it basis a frog will occasionally seize a fish. It is the result of a short-sighted blunder with no harm intended but the strength of the frog's grip is such that the effect on the fish is likely to be fatal. The cases I have been able to investigate personally occurred in abnormal conditions: ponds shrunk by drought, exceptional numbers of frogs (presumably because some spawning sites were completely dried out) and fish with no deep water to escape to. So there is a risk, but in normal conditions it is so slight as to be negligible.

The tadpoles that emerge from the masses of frog spawn, and the ropes of jelly laid by toads, are as welcome to the pond-owner as they are to all the carnivores in the pond. Large numbers of tadpoles are eaten by fish, dragonfly nymphs, diving beetles and their larvae, leeches, and even by each other. In the meantime they are busy eating algae, decaying plants, drowned worms, surplus fishfood and

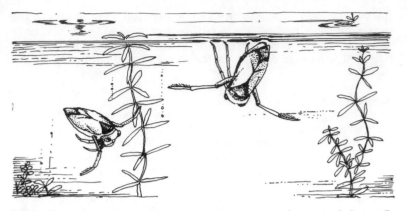

Water Boatmen prey on aquatic creatures up to the size of dragonfly nymphs, Dytiscus *larvae, and small fish. They can be netted when they rise to the surface to take in a fresh supply of air.*

practically every kind of organic pond rubbish. They give the pond a thorough spring clean. More than any other creatures tadpoles genuinely deserve to be called scavengers.

6
Pondside Planting

This is an appropriate point at which to consider, as promised earlier, the question of a bog garden. Such a feature is not without difficulties, and the first is that 'bog plants' is a very misleading description for the plants to which it is traditionally applied. You would expect the term to embrace plants which like growing in a bog, such as Bog Bean (*Menyanthes*), Bog Arum (*Calla palustris*), Bog Daisy (Yorkshire for *Caltha palustris*), Cotton Grass (*Eriophorum*) and Flag Iris (*I. pseudacorus*), among many others. These we have already met, however; they are on the marginal shelf, their toes in saturated soil barely covered with water, and confined in their separate containers to stop them from mixing and choking each other. These true bog plants are already catered for, as marginals. Clearly there is no need to create for them a separate entity and call it a bog garden.

In fact 'bog plants' is the term traditionally applied to Astilbes, Primulas, *Iris sibirica*, and other plants which like plenty of moisture, but would not survive in a genuine bog. Their roots need soil containing air as well as moisture, whereas true bog plants are adapted to grow in saturated soil without air. The waterline is the great divide between the two types. In the days of large country houses with lakes and streams, Primulas and Irises and Astilbes were planted in masses at the waterside, above water level but able to send feeding roots down in summer to unlimited moisture. They are waterside plants, not bog plants, and I shall call them waterside plants from now on.

The vast majority of ponds nowadays have impervious linings of concrete or plastic, completely separating the water in the pond from the soil outside it. How, then, can satisfactory conditions be created for the cultivation of waterside plants? One solution to the problem is to create, as part of the over-all pond design, and within the limits of the concrete shell or plastic liner, a wide shallow area; in effect, a marginal shelf several feet wide. On this, soil is built up at least 6 inches above water level, preferably varying between 6 and 12 inches. A retaining wall must be created, not too high to prevent water from the pond seeping into the soil, and stout enough to hold the soil. If the retaining wall proves inadequate – as often seems to happen after a year or two – things can get very messy. Even so, it is a better idea than the one which relies on overfilling the pond periodically so that water overflows to soak the soil alongside. This can be rejected out of hand, not only because the soaking tends to be erratic and inadequate, but because the frequent flushing of water through the pond plays havoc with pond temperature and balance.

The best arrangement, I believe, is to make an area for waterside plants alongside the pond as a separate unit, close enough to seem part of it, but having no connection with the pond. The area is formed with a liner, as if you were making a shallow pond to be filled with soil instead of water. The main differences are that the liner is turned up at the sides but does not need to reach the surface so there is no flap of spare material to secure and disguise; and that the liner is not expected to hold water. The aim will not be to prevent drainage altogether, which could result in sour soil, just to slow it down. The method is to excavate about 12 inches of soil (which will be returned, so do not move it too far) and to lay down a liner which will cover the bottom and come roughly two-thirds of the way up the sides. There are no niceties here as to exact depth or angle of slope on the sides. Any liner material will do, but since polythene is entirely satisfactory there is no need to purchase anything more expensive. An old, damaged, pond liner of any kind is ideal. There must be holes: if necessary make them with a garden fork. Return half of the soil you excavated, well mixed with peat and either rotted cow manure or compost. Then install the irrigation system, in the shape of $\frac{3}{4}$-inch or 1-inch i.d. plastic tubing (PVC hose will do very well since it is going to be buried) drilled with $\frac{1}{8}$-inch or $\frac{3}{16}$-inch holes at 6-inch intervals.

One end must be firmly capped or plugged. Lay the tubing down the middle and bring the uncapped end up above the surface and fit a plastic hose connector. Then return the rest of the soil mixture. The level of the finished bed will be little more (by the amount of peat and manure added) than the level of adjacent soil, and of the water on the other side of the pond surround. This is aesthetically more satisfying than the raised mound that inevitably results from the extended marginal shelf arrangement previously described. By connecting a hose to the projecting end of the buried tubing the bed can be given a thorough soaking as often as is needed. This will only be during the growing season; in winter too much moisture can be damaging, hence the need for the drainage holes in the liner.

Waterside Plants

Primulas, Irises and Astilbes are all you need to produce a superbly colourful flower display in the moist-soil bed from April to August.

The primula succession starts in April with the intense carmine pink of 6-inch high *P. rosea* Delight and both white and violet forms of the drumstick primula, *P. denticulata*. In May begins the cavalcade of primulas with tiers of flowers that are collectively referred to as candelabra types. *P. japonica* has luxuriant leaf rosettes and 2-foot spires of crimson, pink or white flowers. *P. pulverulenta*, 2 to 3 feet, has mealy stems and deep crimson flowers; the Bartley strain of this species is possibly the finest of all the candelabras, with lovely shades of pale salmon and shell pink. *P. chungensis*, $1\frac{1}{2}$ feet, has more vivid orange flowers. Many of these go on flowering into June, when they are joined by other candelabras. *P. aurantiaca*, 12 inches, is reddish orange; *P. bulleyana*, 18 inches, has rich yellow flowers; *P. prolifera*, 18 inches, is a shorter version of the splendid golden yellow 3-foot *P. helodoxa* (**52**); and *P.* Asthore hybrids, $1\frac{1}{2}$ to 2 feet, include shades of yellow, apricot, flame, pink and mauve. Primulas of the cowslip type include the 2-foot lemon yellow *P. sikkimensis* that flowers in May, and the July flowering 3-foot giant *P. florindae*.

The flower spectacular in June is enhanced by two groups of Iris. *I. sibirica*, in numerous blue, white or purple varieties, makes rushy 3 to 4-foot clumps that can enlarge rapidly given ample summer moisture. *I. kaempferi* (**54**), which needs acid soil, has larger flowers in many shades and mixtures of blue, purple, mauve, lilac and white.

The ornamental value of Astilbes begins in April with the new purplish or bronzy green deeply cut foliage. Flowering runs from June into August. Among many fine varieties Red Sentinel, Cologne (deep pink), Bressingham Beauty (soft pink) and Deutschland (white) are outstanding. Fanal (red), Intermezzo (salmon) and Mainz (rose lilac) are shorter growers to about 2 feet.

Among these vivid displays of bloom, the relief of some primarily foliage plants is not unwelcome. *Hosta sieboldi*, *H. undulata variegata* and *H. crispula* (**55**) have bold attractive leaves which enhance the oasis-like character of a water garden. *Rodgersia* (**53**) and ferns such as *Osmunda regalis* (**50**) offer variety in form and texture. One waterside plant that can hardly be ignored is the magnificent *Gunnera manicata* (**51**). It has to be mentioned if only to point out that it is not suitable for artificial moisture beds or small-scale water gardens. The place for it is a 50-foot stretch of bank beside a lake or stream where its massive cluster of 8 to 10-foot wide leaves is in scale with the surroundings.

The same can be said for the weeping willow, a tree which is all too often the first thing to be planted beside a small garden pond. The consequences can only be disastrous. Within a very few years the tree casts not only unwelcome shade, but a rain of twigs and leaves that chokes the water with rubbish and kills all the fish. Leave willows to grace the banks of lakes in public parks where they belong.

Dry Margins

Not all gardeners share that streak of perversity that insists on labouring to grow certain plants in conditions that cannot be made congenial without a good deal of effort. If the soil around an artifical pond is not right for waterside plants, they ask, why not grow something else? They have a point. Let us suppose, then, that the soil around the pond gets no moisture from it; it is plain average soil and, since the pond was deliberately sited to get all the sun possible, it may well be on the dry side of average. This will be particularly true of soil built up to make a rockery and watercourse because it will not only be better drained but sloped to catch the full effect of the sun as well. Here any of the usual sun-loving rockery plants can be grown. Among the most useful in this context are the trailing and spreading types whose growth complements the flow of water over the cascade ledges: bright pink *Saponaria*, for example, and blue-flowered *Campanula* Birch Hybrid. Alpine Phlox such as Violet Queen, Blue Ridge, Emerald Cushion (blue) and Temiscaming (crimson) make sheets of colour. *Geranium subcaulescens splendens* (57) and the pink *G. dalmaticum* are invaluable. *Minuartia verna caespitosa aurea* is a gem for making a moss-like carpet of yellow foliage particularly where there may be just an occasional splash of spray from the waterfall.

Some shrubs can be useful too. *Cotoneaster* Gnome and *C. dammeri* make prostrate growth flow over rockwork and can cover quite an area. Helianthemums are dwarf evergreen shrubs that produce multitudes of flowers through the summer: orange, yellow, carmine, pink, scarlet, copper – there are scores of varieties. They are ideal for a dry border beside the pool. *Cistus*, too, love a sunbaked spot. *C. lusitanicus decumbens* (56), a low spreading bush, produces a long succession of maroon-centred white flowers.

More valuable even than these summer flowering plants are those that brighten things up in the winter, when the pond is looking rather bleak. The ideal plants for this purpose are winterflowering heathers. *Erica carnea* varieties Eileen Porter (carmine), Pink Spangles, Springwood White, Springwood Pink, Ruby Glow, Vivelli (carmine), and hybrids Arthur Johnson (deep pink), Darley Dale (mauve pink),

Furzey (deep rose) and Silver Beads (white) will between them provide a show of flowers from October until Marsh Marigolds are in full bloom in April. They are of alpine origin and extremely hardy. Either acid or limey soil will suit them. With their help the water garden will not altogether lack cheerful colour even in the bleakest winter months.

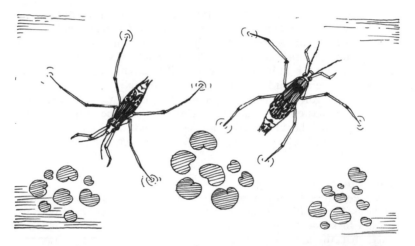

Among the first insects to colonise a new pond are Water Skaters. They live entirely on top of the surface film where they devour any tiny insects that fall onto it. There are several species, ranging in size from grains of soot up to almost an inch in length, and all are harmless.

7
Pond Management and Maintenance

This chapter is not about problems, pests and diseases; not exclusively anyway. It is about a variety of things that may happen as a water garden matures, some desirable and welcome, some inevitable and requiring routine attention, and some that really are problems. Of the last, many are unlikely to crop up if the water garden has been properly designed and constructed, and sensibly stocked; they are mentioned in the following pages for the benefit of gardeners who may have inherited problems created by others. Some of the 'happenings' are seasonal, but not all. They will be best dealt with according to whether they affect the pond fabric, the water, the plants, or the fish.

The Pond Structure

Damage to the structural fabric of the pond is sometimes immediately obvious. If you fall into a liner pond and try to save yourself with the garden fork you happen to be carrying, you will know at once not only that the liner has been punctured, but exactly where the punctures are. More often it is an abnormal rate of water loss that gives the first hint of something being amiss. That raises the question of what is normal. Water loss by evaporation is to be expected but it varies considerably with climatic conditions and what is normal will depend on where you live. Humidity makes a great deal of difference and so does air movement. Evaporation loss may be noticeable in a dry sunny spell; if there is also a steady wind the loss rate will increase dramatically as the wind speed increases. There is no reason, incidentally, why tap water should not be used to make good evaporation loss: the quantity will be small in relation to the volume in the pond and the effect of cold chlorinated tap water in this context will not be significant.

Normal evaporation loss, then, is something only you can judge from experience. If there is greater loss than evaporation would seem to account for, a leaking pond is not the only cause to be suspected. If there is a waterfall system, the first thing to do is to switch off the pump. If water loss stops when the pump is off the leak is in the watercourse; all the water that is being pumped up is not getting back to the pond. If it is an old concrete watercourse soil settlement has no doubt opened cracks between concrete and natural stone. There is no cure for this, short of rebuilding the whole thing: see Chapter 3. However, the problem may not be structural. If, when the pump is off, the pools and channels remain full of water, it argues that the loss may be occurring only when the water is on the move. Examine it closely in operation. Is water splashing over the side? Is water dribbling back under sills and finding its way out of the system, instead of pouring cleanly from one step to the next? Has plant growth intruded from the adjoining rockery? The amount of water that can be lost by splashing off leaves or running down plant stems into the surrounding soil is quite remarkable.

If water loss continues when the waterfall pump is not in operation it has to be assumed that the pond itself is leaking. The only way to discover where is to let the level fall until it stops, and then to examine the fabric closely along the settled waterline. If the leak is in the bottom, of course, all the water will be lost, and this raises the question of what to do with the fish while the leak is being repaired. Advice about temporary housing for fish and plants will be found later in this chapter. Techniques for repairing leaks depend on the nature of the pond fabric.

Repairing concrete ponds

The repair technique adopted for a concrete pond will depend on the cause of the trouble. If the concrete is porous (because the wrong proportions have been used in the mix, or mixing has not been thorough) it should be possible to remedy this by applying to the whole surface a latex grout well brushed in, or a layer of cement/sand latex mortar well bonded to the base concrete. Alternatively, a liquid plastic pond paint (and it must be one made specifically for the purpose) should solve the problem, for a year or two at least.

The situation is different if the pool is cracked. This might be the result of heavy ice exerting pressure against vertical walls or of the seasonal expansion and contraction of a clay soil. In either case further movement can be expected to occur and neither a rigid cementatious type of repair nor a skin of paint would be able to prevent cracks from re-opening. In this case there is only one satisfactory long-term answer and that is to line the pond with one of

137

the flexible sheet plastic materials described in Chapter 2. They can stretch to accommodate any future movement of the concrete shell. For the sake of long-term peace of mind this is also the best way to solve the problem of porous concrete.

The installation of a liner in a concrete pond can present problems because something has to be done with a flap of spare material round the edge. It may involve removing and then replacing on top of the liner flap both paving stones and part at least of any rockery built along the edge. If there is only flat paving it is possible to lay the liner flap on top of it and then bed another course of paving on top of that, but because of the projection of the original paving this is the less satisfactory alternative.

The pond must be cleared of any debris before installing the liner in the manner described in Chapter 2, the greatest care being taken to avoid the liner being dragged over any rough concrete. In the case of a rectangular pond a slightly different technique is required. Lay the liner on the floor, centrally placed so that there is the same amount of surplus all round. Run the water and, standing barefoot in the pond, use hands and feet to smooth out wrinkles. Helpers standing at the pond edge who can give the liner a heave this way or that will help to discourage folding except in the corners. With a couple of inches of water on the bottom there is no danger whatever that they will shift the liner's position. Smooth the liner towards the corners and mitre-fold it, tucking surplus material behind the vertical corner fold. When the pond is full, cut away the folded spare material at each corner (but do not cut the notch right to the waterline) to allow the rest of the flap to lie flat.

Repairing glassfibre ponds
Leaks in glassfibre ponds are rare but may result either from careless installation on an uneven base with projecting stones, or from excessively weighty rockery stones splitting the rim. Repair is with resin, mixed with catalyst, brushed onto layers of glassfibre mat over the damaged area. A glassfibre repair kit (as used for patching damaged vehicle bodies or glassfibre boat hulls) contains all the necessary ingredients.

Repairing PVC liners
This is where you will be glad that you saved the spare material trimmed off the liner when the pond was made. Punctures and tears are no problem. The area to be repaired must be clean and dry. Apply a suitable PVC adhesive (e.g. Bostik No 1) to the area, and to a PVC

patch, give it a minute or two to become tacky, and press the patch firmly into place. Keep some pressure on it if possible. After an hour the pond can be refilled. A similar technique can be applied to an elderly PVC liner that has become flaky and brittle from years of exposure to the sun above water level. The chance of success is not great because there is not much for the patch to bond to, but it is worth a try. Alternatively replace the liner. There is nothing that can be painted onto an old porous liner to prevent leaks.

Repairing butyl rubber liners
Butyl is not easily damaged but children can do it with determination and sharp sticks. Butyl retailers usually sell a sticky tarry-looking repair tape that is as awkward to handle as flypaper, but does the job. Pond patching kits for both PVC and butyl ponds are sold in Britain; be careful to specify the material you want it for or you may get the one that does not work on your liner.

Repairing polythene liners
Nothing effective can be done to repair torn or brittle polythene liners, which is one of the reasons why they are not recommended for pond construction.

Damage by roots
I have often been told about – and sometimes shown – ponds which appear to have been damaged by the roots of trees. I still do not believe that tree roots represent any danger to a sound pond. The soil immediately outside the pond shell, particularly when there is a paved surround, tends to be drier, if anything, than the rest of the area. There is less likelihood of tree roots exploring this area than others. Even if they did, can it seriously be supposed that a tree root somehow divines that there is water on the other side of a concrete pond shell and sets out to drill a hole through it? What actually happens, of course, is that the pond, for one of the several reasons concrete ponds have for doing so, begins to leak. Now there is moisture in the soil outside the shell and tree roots develop in that direction to exploit it. The growing tip of a root, infinitely small, explores a hairline crack in the concrete, and expands, and grows further, and expands. Eventually, of course, the pond really empties out, revealing the now substantial crack in the concrete with roots growing through it. The roots get the blame, naturally enough. They made the initial damage worse, certainly, but they did not start it. The leak came first.

The Water
The water in a pond swarms with a myriad of microscopic organisms. Of the vast majority the pond-owner is blissfully unaware. Those that he cannot fail to notice (and that often irritate him to the point of desperation) are the ones that discolour the water. Not that he has any right to expect the glittering transparency of a pond newly filled with chlorinated tap water to persist indefinitely. As it becomes increasingly fit to support life it will develop the slightest tint of pale amber. This is entirely as it should be, and as long as it stays like that the pond-owner is content. Let it become increasingly murky and discoloured, however, and he tends to panic and worry, assuming that 'something has gone wrong'. In some cases it might be true; nine times out of ten it means nothing of the kind. In order to know which, it is only necessary to observe the colour of the water.

Green water
Green water is caused by single-celled free-swimming algae. They are individually microscopic but may be present in such numbers as to make the pool look as if it is filled with green distemper. They depend for existence on light and mineral salts, both of which are abundantly available in a newly filled pond in which plant growth is still relatively undeveloped. So it is entirely natural for the new pond to be pea-soup green within a week or two of being filled. If manure or fertiliser is used, the nutrients dissolving out will give that much more encouragement for the algae, and it will take longer for the water to clear. Nevertheless, clear it will if submerged oxygenators and surface covering plants are present in the sort of numbers discussed in Chapter 4. The surface cover of water lily and other leaves cuts off sunlight at the surface; nutrients dissolved in the water are consumed in building up the growth of oxygenators. Single-celled algae swarming in the upper water layers where light intensity and warmth are greatest begin to find things difficult. Starved of food and deprived of light they die and sink to the bottom. The water clears, and it very often happens abruptly, overnight. It may have taken 3 weeks or 3 months to achieve that happy state. There is no 'normal' period for this; it depends on so many variables – water chemistry, soil richness, plant density, seasonal weather – that it is different for every pond. Changing the water will not help to accelerate the process; it only introduces a fresh supply of mineral salts and puts you back to square one, with the whole process to go through again. The recipe for clear water is simply plants and patience.

Once the water has cleared it should stay that way except, perhaps, for a brief outbreak in spring. For one reason and another (including the dead algae that sank) there is always a mulm of mineral-rich sediment on the bottom. In winter the top water layer becomes cold, sinks, and forces the richer bottom layer of water upwards. This results in nutrients being present in the upper water layers to nourish a fresh outburst of algae when warmer weather occurs in the spring. It lasts only until the new season's growth of oxygenators and lilies gets going.

What happens, however, if there is a constant stirring of the water, carrying minerals from the bottom into the warm bright upper layers? The result is a continuous process of algae production so that the pool never properly clears. Exactly this effect can be produced by fish constantly working over the bottom. In very small ponds a few big old fish can be responsible for permanently green water. Currents which continuously upset the balance of the pool can also be the result of overdoing the moving water effects, or failing to site the pump so that disturbance is minimised, as described in Chapter 3. The smaller the pond the more susceptible it will be to imbalance from these causes.

Green water problems are inherent in some pond designs. If the pond is a shallow saucer, or has a very large shallow-water area and a small area only of deeper water, then the volume will be small in relation to the surface area and algae of one sort or another will be a constant headache unless the surface is almost completely covered. Sometimes it is necessary to look beyond the pond itself to discover the cause of persistently green water. In one stubborn case it was eventually realised that the contours of the garden encouraged surface water to run into the pond and, since the adjacent lawn was dressed regularly with fertiliser, the pond was a soup of plant nutrients in which algae would never starve. Had the lawn fertiliser been mixed with weedkiller the results would have been much worse: all the pond plants and fish would have been killed.

Cures for green water

As has been said, plants and patience are the answer to green water. Some people do not have the patience; they want immediate results and feel sure there must be something that they can pour into the pond out of a bottle that will provide an instant solution. For them there are indeed products, such as Algizin A or Aquaclear, that will do the trick. Or they can mix their own, in the form of a quarter of a teaspoonful of potassium permanganate crystals for every 200 gallons of pond water dissolved in half a gallon of water. Algicides do not change the basic conditions which encourage algae. Their effect is temporary and the dose has to be repeated at frequent intervals to maintain the improvement. They do not hasten the day when the pond will be naturally clear. Copper sulphate is not recommended: it works, but it is only too easy to overdose and kill your cherished pond plants as well as the algae. Hydrated lime works in some ponds and has disastrous effects in others. Success requires particular conditions of water chemistry, including pH, and if the conditions are not right all fish in the pond roll over and expire.

If partial surface cover discourages algae why not carry the idea to its logical conclusion? Yes, if the pond is covered with boards and/or polythene so that light is totally excluded the algae will die. So will any pond plants, eventually, but not before fish are killed by the overproduction of carbon dioxide. This trick works only if the pond contains nothing but water and algae.

Natural control of green water can be achieved rather neatly (even though temporarily) by removing all the fish and introducing a quantity of *Daphnia*. These so-called water fleas are tiny crustaceans sold by many pet shops as fish food. They will feed and increase on a diet of free-swimming algae. Once the water is clear the fish can be returned to make a feast of the *Daphnia*. Freshwater mussels are filter feeders quite capable of clearing the water by straining out all the algae. Unfortunately they like to plough around in a continuous mud layer and the larval form of some species is parasitic for a time on fish. When they exhaust the food supply mussels have a habit of dying and, in the process of decay, creating problems worse than the one they were introduced to solve.

Red water

I have occasionally seen ponds with water so red as to hint at some dire tragedy. In fact, the alarming colour was just another manifestation of algal growth. After a week or so it declined to a brown sediment on the bottom and in a month was no more than a memory.

Brown water

Murky brown water is the result of muddy sediment being stirred up by fish or by water turbulence. It may well have a greenish component because such stirring tends to encourage algal growth. The brown colour comes from fine particles of inorganic matter in suspension in the water. These are not affected by algicides, but Acurel, a useful product that flocculates any floating particles of both organic and inorganic matter and deposits it on the bottom, will clear the water. Not for long, of course, if something is not done about the causes of stirring and turbulence.

Black water
Inky black water, usually occurring in winter or early spring, results from a heavy accumulation of tree leaves in the pond. The decay of this material burdens the water with toxic by-products which, if sealed under a sheet of ice, can kill the fish. Even if it does not come to that, the toxins create an unhealthy environment in which fish will be vulnerable to fungus and other disease organisms. Black water indicates the need for at least a partial water change and later a complete spring clean (see p. 157), and for prevention next autumn in the shape of anti-leaf netting; the plastic netting sold for protecting soft fruits is very satisfactory.

Milky water
Milky clouded water indicates decay and water pollution. It arises from the decomposition of organic matter, particularly of fleshy origin. Change the water, and search for the source of the trouble; it may turn out to be dead fish or dead mussels or a drowned hedgehog. The overgenerous use of bonemeal can sometimes produce the same effect.

Oil and dust
A film of oil, revealed by rainbow streaks on the water surface, often occurs in the autumn. It comes from the decay of water lily leaves. It can be removed easily by laying a sheet of newspaper on the water and drawing it off after only a few seconds. The same method can be used to remove fine dust, pollen and other particles too light to sink through the surface film.

Water changes
It will be seen that water changing, though never the answer to green water problems, becomes necessary if the water is polluted. Whether the water is poisoned by decaying organic matter or by the accidental introduction of insecticide or weedkiller, there is no question of pouring in an antidote; a water change is the only answer. Cold chlorinated water is far from ideal, but in this situation it has to be regarded as the lesser of two evils. Its effects can be made less harsh by running it in very slowly, and by adding Haloex or a similar dechlorinator. There are two ways of doing a water change. One is to run a trickling hose into the pond, letting the water mix and

overflow; after several hours (or even a day or two depending on size) the original water will have been substantially replaced, or at least well diluted. The difficulty occurs in knowing to what extent. The alternative is to pump or syphon out a specific fraction, say a half or a third of the pool volume, then run water in slowly to fill up. Either way fish can remain in the pond; the slow trickling introduction of tap water is for their benefit, to ensure that the temperature change in the water is very gradual.

Severe chemical pollution by insecticides/weedkillers or (children being what they are) by detergents, paint, creosote and the like, calls not only for a water change but for replanting in completely new soil.

Even though it suffers none of these unhappy accidents, the water in a small pond that is overstocked with fish, as small ponds usually are, can get rather stale and mildly poisonous. Fish deplete trace elements as they grow, and they constantly excrete waste products, not all of which are converted by bacteria into useful plant food. There is a gradual build-up of toxicity and an increasing risk of disease. This undesirable state of affairs can be avoided by giving the pond a half water change every spring. It is possible to make out a case for doing the same thing in the autumn too. Obviously there is a risk of losing hard-won pond balance and suffering green water again for a time, but that is a minor nuisance compared with the dangers that arise in a small overstocked pond from fish swimming around in their own wastes.

The Plants
Started off in containers of suitable size and with a satisfactory soil mixture, as described in Chapter 4, aquatic plants normally make rapid headway. If there is a problem it is more likely to be of too much rather than too little growth. Container planting is particularly valuable in curbing such aggressive explorers as *Ranunculus lingua* and the *Typhas*, and making it easy to spot and sever wandering roots.

Insect pests
Through the summer the foliage of lilies and marginals will suffer blemishes from the attentions of various insects. Most are of no great significance, which is just as well since the spraying of insecticides is ruled out by the presence of fish. The holes cut by China Marks Moth caterpillars are common but unimportant. The activities of Water Lily Beetles are damaging but uncommon, and easily dealt with by removing affected leaves complete with beetles, larvae and eggs. A

more common nuisance is caused by a midge which lays its eggs on the floating leaves of aquatics. The larvae eat away the leaf tissue and heavy attacks can be crippling. Large lilies with thick tough leaves are not troubled but the thin-leaved pygmy and small lilies can have their leaves reduced to nothing but veins; the damage may be fatal to young plants. The larvae burrowing in the leaf are slender, transparent and very difficult to see, but the way they skeletonise the leaf is unmistakable. Picking off affected leaves may be enough. If all the leaves are attacked as fast as they are produced the only remedy is to lift the plant and immerse it for an hour in a bucket containing insecticide diluted to a strength suitable for spraying greenfly on roses. The lily must than be rinsed in clean water before being returned to the pond. The presence of active small fish such as Golden Orfe, or even Sticklebacks, is some help in combating this nuisance.

In the latter part of the summer, water plants may suffer from 'blackfly', or plum aphids, particularly if there are plum trees (their alternative host plant) in the vicinity. Old water lilies with upstanding overcrowded leaves are particularly prone to infestation since they give the aphids cover and protection from predators. Hosing the aphids off the leaves into the water where fish can pick them off works to some extent if repeated daily, but on the whole aphids are a cross that has to be borne.

Increasing the stock
The crowded leaves of hardy water lilies pushed high above the surface are occasionally the result of a very vigorous variety being planted in unsuitable shallow water. Much more commonly it is simply the result of the plant being left undivided for too long. The remedy is to lift the lily, preferably in the earlier part of the growing season, and to split it up. It requires strength and a sharp blade to cut into an old woody rhizome; do not be squeamish. Where to apply the knife, and how many pieces, each with its own sprout of leaves and roots, can be got out of the old crown, is not easy to describe, but I promise that it will become obvious the moment you wash the mud away from the lifted plant. Throw away the oldest part of the crown and plant up as many of the young offsets as you need.

The failure of water lilies to flower freely may be due to one of several causes, or possibly a combination. Water lilies are discouraged from flowering by cold water; by inadequate sunshine; by being planted too deep in the soil; by being in too great a depth of water; by moving currents; and by starvation.

If the plant is starved the only entirely satisfactory solution is to replant it in fresh soil. The next best answer is to insert pellets of nutrients into the existing soil. They might be balls of clay mixed with coarse bonemeal. I prefer two or three Phostrogen Plantoids encased in a ball of clay; three such balls pushed down among the roots of a starved lily will have a tonic effect. Two such applications in the course of a growing season are recommended.

Most marginal plants soon make substantial clumps and many of them have expansive tendencies. It pays to examine them closely at least once a year. Lift out the container and cut back superfluous roots and shoots. If overfilled, turn out the plant, split it up, and replant with new soil.

By the late summer most oxygenators will have made masses of growth which will have served its purpose. Its natural fate, from August onward, is simply to die back and decay and we do not want that to happen in the pond, especially if it is a small one. So during August, or by mid-September at the latest, I strongly recommend cutting back to a few inches the growth of *Anacharis*, *Elodea*, *Myriophyllum*, *Potamogeton* and *Ranunculus aquatilis*. This does no more than anticipate the natural pruning that autumn cold would perform, and it helps to avoid the accumulation of decaying organic matter in the pond.

In areas where there is no natural pruning by frost, this cutting back helps to get rid of long stringy shoots and encourage new growth from the base. Cutting back is far better than merely hauling out, but only the latter is feasible in the case of *Ceratophyllum*, of which some fragments need to be left to start things off next season. Patches of *Callitriche* and *Hottonia*, which look particularly attractive in the autumn, should be excepted from this operation.

The spent leaves and flowers of water lilies should also be removed as far as is practicable, at least from August onward. Once the foliage of marginal plants is browned with frost they should be cut down to water level and removed so that they do not collapse and decay in the water.

Plant growth may appear in the pond in the unwelcome form of filamentous algae. Indeed it can be said that filamentous algae in one form or another will be bound to turn up. It may be as fine hairs on plant stems and leaves or the furry growth that often develops on the walls of the pond. These are of no great moment and are often unnoticed. The form which makes itself very evident is known as silkweed or blanketweed because the very long threads are smooth to the touch, and can form such tangled masses as to swamp other plant growth. Blanketweed is a simple form of plant life. It contains chlorophyll and, in daylight, produces oxygen. It is normally associated with very clear water. It can be tolerated in moderation and indeed it is impossible to eradicate all forms of filamentous algae entirely. Elaborate precautions to prevent its introduction to a pond by sterilising all new plants will not prevent it from arriving in the form of airborne spores. If conditions are favourable there is nothing you can do to keep it out; but you can control it by making the conditions as unfavourable as possible. Blanketweed and the green specks that produce 'pea-soup' water are both algae. In one case, individual mobile cells wander in the water: in the other, cells are joined to form long green strands. Both are algae, however, thriving on light and mineral nutrients. Everything that has been said about the origins and control of green water (pp. 140–1) applies equally to blanketweed. Leaves on the surface, cutting off sunlight, are the most important factor in control.

In the case of blanketweed there is also the possibility of manual control. A rake can be used to comb it out of the oxygenators. A rough stick twisted among the mass of strands will draw threads from all over the pond. It is fascinating to see what it brings with it in the way of snails, beetles, newts, fry and assorted insect larvae. Since both snails and goldfish include some algal growth in their diets they ought in theory to keep the stuff in check. In practice they cannot be seen to make any difference. As an emergency measure in cases of severe infestation I have found 'Algacadabra' and similar pond blocks, and Algizin P to be effective in killing blanketweed. Close attention to the product instructions is essential: overdosing may damage the pond plants. It must be remembered that masses of decaying blanketweed can de-oxygenate the water and imperil the fish so that the manual removal of as much of the weed as possible is essential both before and after chemical treatment. Light control by improved surface cover is, of course, the best long-term answer to blanketweed.

The Fish

It happens every year but many pond-owners fail to recognise it for what it is. 'I thought all these fish were supposed to live happily together', they tell me. 'Well there's one that's being attacked by the others. They are chasing it and shoving it and giving it a terrible time. Are they trying to push it out of the pond? Why are they picking on that one? How can I stop it?'

Allowing for a bit of exaggeration that is not a bad description of what happens when a female goldfish is close to spawning and eager males are jockeying for position to fertilise the eggs by discharging

147

milt into the water as the female sheds her eggs among the aquatic plants. It does not look very friendly but it is no more than the normal spawning ritual. The female is not being attacked, of course, and there is no reason to interfere with the process. Given a number of goldfish, of whatever varieties, there is almost bound to be a mixture of sexes. With sexually mature fish (which very roughly speaking means 3 years old or more, and 4 to 5 inches or more), well fed and in well-oxygenated water, spawning is bound to occur.

To improve the survival chances of fertilised eggs it is necessary to remove them to a safer place. Fish prefer to spawn among plants in shallow water, and plastic seed trays thickly planted with oxygenators and standing on a marginal shelf provide ideal conditions. Once spawning is complete the tray can be lifted gently, very gently, from the pond. This is where a second pond proves a great boon. It will, of course, contain no fish. It should be planted and contain mature water, which means it may also have been colonised by beetles, water boatmen and other potential insect predators. Constant vigilance will be necessary to net these out. Hatching should take place in four to six days if the temperature is around 70°F (21°C), and longer if it is cooler. Once the fry have consumed their yolk sacs they will feed on tiny organisms occurring naturally in the water. Special fry food, or even ordinary flake food crumbled fine, will assist rapid growth, so that by autumn they will have reached the $1\frac{1}{2}$ to 2 inches considered necessary to survive the winter outdoors.

Some of the fry will be coloured from the start; some will be dark and drab but gradually develop colour; and some will stay un-coloured, like the one visible on plate **36**. Since goldfish are coloured sports from an originally drab olive species some reversion is to be expected and selection is necessary to keep the coloured strain. Weed out any fish that are still drab by the time they are 18 months old or 3 inches long. Colour in goldfish is not a fixed characteristic and the extent of black markings, for example, on a red fish can increase or decrease with age.

Fish ailments

Well-nourished fish in a well-managed pond have strong natural resistance to the potentially harmful organisms (fungus spores and bacteria, for example) that always surround them. Continuing health depends more than anything else on keeping the water free from pollution. Pollution may arise from such varied causes as an excess of decaying vegetation, insecticide spraydrift, fish wastes in an over-crowded pond, laburnum flowers or seeds, weedkiller washed off the

Green Tench, dark in colour and shy in temperament, are seldom visible. Their reputation as 'doctor fish' and as scavengers is largely undeserved.

lawn, and a build-up of carbon dioxide in thundery weather. The water may look perfect but still be poisoned. That is why a slow water change is often a necessary part of the treatment for disease problems.

It used to be said that a sick fish was a dead fish, and that was not far wrong. Nowadays there are many effective treatments. The basic difficulty is in diagnosing the problem so that the appropriate remedy can be used.

Since the fish cannot tell us where it hurts diagnosis must depend on intelligent observation by the owner, particularly of behaviour and appearance before death. Once dead a fish is rapidly attacked by saprophytic fungi and other agents of decomposition. In a matter of hours it may look as if it is wearing a woolly coat; this creates the impression that it was killed by fungus infection, which in fact only attacks live fish, whereas the saprophytic fungus only grows on dead creatures. The woolly coat also masks other external symptoms so that, unless pathological laboratory facilities are available, a dead fish very seldom tells us much about why it died. However, if the owner has been alert enough to note any abnormalities of appearance or behaviour before death it should be possible, if not to identify the cause precisely, at least to narrow the field to one of several categories – parasite, bacterium, or fungus, for example – for which there are readily available treatments.

In suggesting treatment for some of the commoner and most easily identified fish health problems I shall not mention drugs which the layman would find it difficult to obtain or to measure with the accuracy required for safe use. Proprietary remedies do not indicate what they contain so the names of drugs do not help in that respect either. I shall mention the names of several products of which I have personal experience but it must be emphasised that there are others of doubtless equal worth, and more are arriving as drug companies wake up to the commercial possibilities offered by the very widespread interest nowadays in keeping ornamental fish.

The names mentioned here may not be available where you live, but others will be. The most suitable will be recommended by a local dealer if you can help him to identify the problem by providing not a long dead corpse but a still-live fish or, failing that, with an account of the behaviour of a fish before it died, describing any way in which its appearance, colour, movement, swimming action, feeding or fin carriage differed from normal. And, of course, with details of the size, colour and position of any spots, marks, growths, patches or other visible external signs.

It may be possible (depending on your estimate of the problem) to avoid the need for consultation by using one of two very old-fashioned remedies based on readily available materials. One is salt and the other permanganate of potash, at one time virtually the sole occupants of the pond-owner's medicine chest. With so many modern remedies available they are inclined nowadays to be overlooked. This is a pity, because they can still be extremely useful. Salt is a very effective treatment for flukes, and useful in dealing with fungus, while nothing makes a fish louse anxious to leave its host as urgently as a dip in permanganate.

The effectiveness of any treatment can be influenced by the chemistry of the pond or tap water. This can vary considerably so results can never be completely predictable. The materials, dose rates and treatment techniques mentioned hereafter have generally proved to be safe and effective. It has to be said, though, that it is possible for exceptional conditions (e.g. the presence of metals such as lead, copper or zinc) to produce abnormal reactions and even toxic side effects. Any recommendation of treatment must, therefore, be qualified by a warning to be on the alert, just in case.

Accidents have also been known to occur when miscalculation of gallonage has resulted in heavy overdosing. Individual fish may vary, too, in their tolerance of treatment in the same way that some people can be allergic to drugs that have no adverse effect on others. If, for whatever reason, fish react dramatically to a treatment, the immediate remedy is either to dilute the effect by changing a substantial proportion of the water, or to transfer the fish to untreated water.

Salt treatment

Domestic table salt contains additives to make it run freely and should not be used if sea salt or aquarium salt can be obtained. Treatment is carried out in an aquarium or washing-up bowl and may be prolonged (in the case of fungus infection, for example) or a short dip in a stronger solution.

For a prolonged salt bath use $1\frac{1}{2}$ ounces (3 level tablespoons or 9 level teaspoons) per gallon of water. After three days (or up to six days if the symptoms persist) replace half the salt water with plain water on each of two successive days to readjust the fish gradually to normal water conditions. If the fish appears at the outset to be much weakened, gradually increase and decrease the strength of the solution as follows, using a fresh mixture each day: *1st day* 1 level tablespoon per gallon of water; *2nd day* 2 tablespoons per gallon; *3rd day* 3 tablespoons per gallon; *4th day* 2 tablespoons per gallon; *5th day* 1 tablespoon per gallon; then back to normal water.

For a short bath, if flukes are suspected, use 6 level tablespoons of salt per gallon and leave the fish in it for up to 30 minutes. Be prepared to remove the fish earlier if it shows signs of distress.

Permanganate of potash

Permanganate of potash (*Potassium permanganate*) is an inexpensive material that can be purchased in crystal form from a pharmacist, and has long been used as a pond and aquarium disinfectant. Some claim to have found it effective as a temporary cure for green water, while others maintain that it will cure new concrete and make it harmless. I have some sympathy with the first claim and no faith whatever in the second.

For pond treatment as a general disinfectant, or to treat fungussy fish that cannot be caught, $2\frac{1}{4}$ grams of crystals should be used for every 100 gallons of pond water. If the pond gallonage is known only approximately, use 2 grams per 100 gallons to be on the safe side. The crystals should be dissolved in a gallon or two of water and the solution well distributed in the pond, preferably through a watering can. The purplish discoloration of the water disappears in a day or two.

For a short bath of up to 2 hours in an aquarium or similar container use 45 milligrams per gallon of water.

Fish can be freed of lice (*Argulus*) almost instantaneously by a brief dip (not more than 1 minute) in a solution of 150 milligrams per gallon.

Exceeding the recommended times may result in damage to the fish's gills.

No attempt will be made here to provide an exhaustive list of fish diseases, many of which the layman simply does not have the equipment to identify. The following notes refer only to those problems which an observant pond-owner has a good chance of diagnosing and treating successfully. The remedy, as will be seen, is not always simply a matter of pouring chemicals into the water. The treatment of fish removed from the pond to an aquarium, large domestic bowl, or similar small volume of water, is referred to as 'in-tank treatment'. A suitable 'pond treatment' is specified where such a course is feasible.

Fungus infection

This is a common ailment, and one about which there are many misunderstandings. It is not always appreciated, for example, that the spores of parasitic fungus are present in all water; fish are surrounded by them all their lives. As long as the fish are well-nourished, undamaged, and living in well-oxygenated unpolluted water their resistance to infection is complete. It is when that resistance is undermined that the fungus can gain a hold which may, in time, prove fatal. Fungus infection is always a secondary problem, and a clear indication that there is something else amiss. In addition to treating the fish it is vitally important to discover and correct the conditions that made the fish susceptible to infection. There are many possibilities.

Fish which are weakened by exhaustion after spawning, or after the winter fast, or by polluted water, or by travel stress, or by a drastic temperature change, or by overcrowding, are all likely to develop fungus. So are fish whose protective body coating is weakened by handling, or by the caustic effect of chemicals from cement, or by physical damage. Wounds caused by cats, beetles, birds or leeches are breaches in the fish's defensive coat which allow fungus spores to gain an entry.

They develop into woolly tufts of grey or white on the body or fins. The cotton-wool growths may well be stained green if the fish is swimming in pea-soupy water, making the threads look rather like blanketweed, but in fact there is no connection between the disease and blanketweed.

Fungus is not infectious from fish to fish. A fish which is clawed by a cat is likely to become infected but that fish is no danger to other, undamaged, fish in the pond.

However, if a number of fish share the same unhealthy situation (a pond overstocked with overlarge overfed fish, for example) it is likely that they will all develop fungus; but they will not have caught it from each other.

Fungus infection is often a problem in the spring, particularly when night temperatures keep low. The vitality of fish is at its lowest ebb after their winter fast and if low temperatures persist they will not begin to feed and build up their resistance. In very cold springs there may be fatalities, and very little can be done to help. Throwing food into the pond when the fish have no inclination to feed simply places them under the additional stress of living in polluted water. Live food in the shape of *Daphnia* (Water Fleas) can be introduced so that when the water does warm up and the fish find their appetites they will also find a nourishing meal waiting for them. If fungus has not gained too strong a hold it is surprising how quickly fish throw it off once they begin to feed heartily.

An outbreak of fungus or whitespot will often follow the cleaning and refilling of the pond when this is done without regard to the shock caused by taking fish out of warm mature water and then replacing them in much colder mains water loaded with chlorine. Any operation involving the transfer of fish from one body of water to another must ensure that any change of temperature will be gradual. The correct procedures are described on pp. 157–9.

While it is vitally important to identify and correct the underlying cause of fungus infection it is possible to treat affected individuals and to save them if the fungus is not too deeply rooted. In-tank treatment with Mycopur is often effective; a salt bath is an older remedy that sometimes works wonders. Fish that cannot be caught can be helped by dosing the pond with Erad-Ich or with potassium permanganate (see p. 151). Any improvement achieved will, of course, be wasted if the underlying cause of the outbreak has not been corrected.

Fungus often invades and obscures the damage done to fin and body tissues by fin rot and other bacterial infections. In such cases treatment should aim at dealing with the basic bacterial problem first (see 'Body deterioration', p. 154).

Since fungus infection is the one disease that nearly every novice fish-keeper has heard of he is inclined to blame it for every blemish that appears on his fish. So fungus treatments are often lavished – with unhappy consequences – on fish that have similar symptoms arising from quite different causes. Not all whitish spots, or patches, or even fungussy-looking growths, are necessarily caused by fungus infection. The other common possibilities, and their remedies, are described in the following paragraphs.

'Mouth fungus'

In spite of its appearance this is not a fungus infection at all, and it is no good treating it as such. The off-white growths in and around the mouth area are caused by *C. columnaris* bacteria. The problem is most likely to occur in unhygienic conditions created by overfeeding or an excess of decaying vegetation. The pond will benefit from a slow water change, if not a complete clean-out, then dosing with Bact-Erad or Myxazin. Infected fish should be given in-tank treatment with Furamor-P or Myxacide.

Body deterioration

This covers an assortment of fairly obvious and easily visible symptoms that are caused by bacteria: they include fin rot, tail rot, body rot, mouth rot, split and frayed fins, ulcers, cloudy eye, mealy off-white body film, peeling body film, buff spots like breadcrumbs, red spots, red patches and bleeding scales. All are infectious.

Pond treatment with Bact-Erad or Myxazin should clear up the trouble but there is likely to be a recurrence if the underlying cause of most bacterial problems, a dirty polluted unhygienic pond, is not corrected by at least a slow water change or, better still, a complete clear-out. Furamor-P, Myxazin, and Bactocide are all valuable for the in-tank treatment of bacterial infections.

Whitespot

Whitespot is a protozoan parasite which causes fish to twitch and flick themselves against the bottom. It is more prevalent in aquaria but can cause trouble in outdoor ponds. Not all white spots, though, indicate the Whitespot parasite. White or whitish spots which appear in some forms of bacterial infection, and also in the early stages of fungus infection, are often diagnosed incorrectly as Whitespot. The use of treatments designed for Whitespot leads to disappointment; they are completely ineffective against bacteria and fungi. The spots of Whitespot can be distinguished by careful examination. They are pure white, $\frac{1}{2}$ to $\frac{1}{4}$ the size of a pinhead, with sharply defined edges. They may occur anywhere on the body, tail or fins.

The life cycle of the parasite makes it easy to eliminate it from the pond provided that all the fish can be removed. Parasites drop from the fish and form cysts from which, in a few hours, several hundred young emerge. They die if they cannot find a host fish within 3 or 4 days. Remove all fish for in-tank treatment with Magicure, Ichcide, or other specific Whitespot cure, giving two doses 48 hours apart. Without fish the pond will certainly be free of parasites after 7 days. If it is not sure that all the fish were caught, dose the pond with Erad-Ich or with Algizin P.

Flukes and crustaceans

Flukes that can seldom be seen with the naked eye may occur in very large numbers on the body and gills, sometimes resulting in small grey vaguely outlined patches that might be taken for a sort of fungus. They cause breathing difficulties, loss of colour, listlessness, pallid gills and sluggish movement. It is only too easy to introduce flukes to a pool, when new fish are added, if the simple precaution of brief treatment in quarantine is neglected. All that is needed is a short bath in a strong salt solution (see 'Salt treatment', p. 151) or in-tank treatment with Sterazin. The treatment of flukes on fish in the pond is feasible with Sterazin-P (if there are no Orfe present) or with Bact-Erad.

A larger parasite, *Argulus* or Fish-louse, is flat, round, light green or brown, up to $\frac{1}{4}$-inch across, and not difficult to see on the fish. It makes fish jump and twitch. The fish-louse is one of the reasons why it is unwise to introduce native fish from the wild; they usually bring *Argulus* with them. The louse has a tenacious grip and is normally very difficult to separate from his host. He will leave immediately, however, if the fish is placed very briefly in a potassium permanganate dip (see p. 152).

The same dip treatment can be tried on another parasite, the Anchor Worm. This appears in the late summer as a thread up to $\frac{3}{4}$-inch long protruding from a small pimple on the fish; two tiny egg-sacks develop on the end. The worms can be removed with tweezers from fish that can be caught; a single drop of neat Myxazin on each worm will serve both to loosen its hold and to disinfect the small wound left by its removal. The treatment of the pond with Sterazin-P, using five doses at intervals of a few days, should ensure that all stages of the parasite are eliminated. A repeat treatment in the following March or April is also recommended. Some caution is required if Orfe are present as they may react badly to this treatment.

Diagnosis uncertain

The obvious debility, droopiness and eventual loss of fish which display no external marks or symptoms can arise from several causes. Such situations can be broadly divided into two categories, the slow and the sudden.

When the process is gradual, fish being lost at intervals, one or two at a time over a period, there must be a strong suspicion that they are suffering either from some form of water pollution or from flukes. All the possible causes of pollution should be considered, and any necessary steps taken to correct them. The commonest are too many fish, too much feeding, and too much decaying rubbish, especially from Willows. Quite small amounts of poisonous materials such as cement dust, the flowers and seeds of Laburnum, and insecticide spraydrift can also produce this effect. In all cases where pollution seems a plausible explanation a water change is called for (see p. 143) and, where there is excessive rubbish, a complete clear-out, as described hereafter. Flukes, a far more widespread cause of general debility than is generally realised, can easily be eliminated from both the fish and the pond by the methods already described.

The sudden death of a number of fish which had seemed to be in good health can only be explained in terms of some very drastic form of pollution rather than disease. The cement dust and insecticide already mentioned can cause sudden death, as can weedkiller washed in from adjoining paths or lawns. Detergents and various other substances may occasionally find their way into garden ponds by accident. There are no 'antidotes'. The only action possible is a complete water change.

Some fish ailments do not respond to present treatments. Dropsy, in which the body becomes bloated, with scales sticking out like a fir cone, is one. Authorities are divided as to whether it is infectious; the immediate destruction of any dropsical fish is recommended. Another problem disease causes deep ulcers like white craters on the fish's body, eating away flesh down to the bone. The cause is not known with certainty, though a combination of bacterial and viral agents has been postulated. For this and some other stubborn bacterial problems the hope of successful treatment depends entirely on the use of antibiotics available only on a veterinarian's prescription. The cost of professional assistance has to be weighed against the value, in terms of sentiment as well as cash, of the fish concerned.

In the unhappy event that a fish has to be destroyed, how is it to be done? It is never a pleasant job but it seems to me that any expedient more concerned with sparing the feelings of the owner than those of the fish is deplorable. I still think that throwing the fish hard against a concrete path, though not very subtle, is the most merciful way of dealing with the problem.

Surface gulping

The mysterious death of numbers of fish, found floating in the morning without a mark on them, is the result not so much of disease as of a meteorological phenomenon. The pond surface normally acts like a lung, taking in oxygen and releasing carbon dioxide. In heavy thundery weather this process may slow down or stop altogether. The result is that carbon dioxide does not escape from the water. As it builds up fish become distressed and mouth at the surface as if gulping air. The effect may be very localised and in intensity it may vary from mild to fatal. It is most critical at night when plants as well as fish are producing carbon dioxide; that is why dead fish are usually found in the morning. Death comes from suffocation by carbon dioxide rather than shortage of oxygen. To add more oxygenating plants (for some people the automatic answer to any pond problem) is no help: at night they only make the problem worse. The answer is not to add oxygen but to get rid of the carbon dioxide and this can be done very easily. All you have to do is agitate the surface of the water. You can stir it with a stick, or churn it up with the jet from a hose; the evening and early morning are the most useful times to do this. If there is a fountain or waterfall no problem need arise; from the time that fish are first seen to be gulping in distress the fountain or waterfall should be run .24 hours a day. If there is no fountain or waterfall an inexpensive aquarium air pump will do for the duration of the emergency, usually no more than a day or two. Such pumps are not designed for use out of doors and need to be housed under cover. Plastic airline will be required, long enough to reach from the pump to the pond. It will terminate in a simple air diffuser which need be only a few inches below the surface. The turbulence created by the scething air bubbles will be enough to keep the fish free from risk.

The Clear-out

The need to empty the pond completely will not arise very often. Except for very small ponds that suffer an abnormally large accumulation of fallen leaves it is not a routine annual necessity. As long as all appears to be well, leave well alone. For most ponds, however, the need for a clear-out arises sooner or later. The early part of the growing season is the best time for it, when the water has warmed up enough to make messing about with water enjoyable. If the clear-out is occasioned by a drastic pollution problem, or the need to repair a leak, the emergency will have to be dealt with when it arises whatever the water temperature.

The first concern is likely to be where to put the fish. If there is a

157

second pond, there is no problem. Indeed, a second pond, not connected to the first, is so useful in such emergencies, as well as for quarantining new fish, isolating and treating sick fish, rearing fry and (at other times) for breeding *Daphnia*, that it should really be designed into the water garden layout from the start. If there is no second pond, there are other possibilities, but the plastic dustbin is not one of them (except perhaps, with 6 inches of water, for two or three small fish); its proportions are wrong. Something relatively shallow with plenty of surface area is needed. The domestic bath will do very well, with 6–8 inches of water in it.

Failing that, you will simply have to knock together a makeshift above-ground pond which can be quickly dismantled once it has served its purpose. This is where inexpensive polythene sheet can prove very useful. The walls of the above-ground temporary pond can be formed with boards or planks on edge, roughly nailed together; ladder sections and bits of hardboard will serve the purpose; even peat bales or bags of soil/sand/fertiliser/whatever can be used (anything, in fact, that will contain the pressure when the cavity is draped with a sheet of PVC or a double thickness of polythene and filled with water). The walls need not be more than 12 inches high. The area should, ideally, be somewhere near the size of the pond being emptied if it is fully stocked with fish. However, assuming that it is not stocked to the limit and that the temporary pond is going to be used for only a few days, it need be only half the area of the original, even less if there is a submersible pump that can be operated in the temporary pond, whether with a fountain jet or an open outlet, to create some surface agitation. Aeration by an aquarium air pump would be beneficial whether the fish are housed in the domestic bath or outdoors.

The temporary quarters should be filled with water from the pond; unless the reason for the clear-out is pollution, in which case tapwater will be used. If Haloex or other dechlorinator is used, fish can be transferred to their temporary quarters 24 hours later; if there is no dechlorinator available wait for three days if circumstances permit.

Netting out the fish is best left until much of the water has been pumped or syphoned out and planting containers removed. Stand the containers in the shade and cover oxygenators, lilies and other surfacing plants with wet newspaper. As fish are netted out examine them closely for any signs of disease or parasites. If the latter are observed, dose the temporary pond with Erad-Ick. If there are no parasites dose with Bact-Erad even if there are no signs of disease. This precaution will guard against the infection of any minor injuries sustained in the process of netting out and transfer. The temporary quarters should be covered with taut small-mesh netting both to keep cats out and Golden Orfe in. If the fountain or waterfall pump is being used to empty the pond make sure that the strainer is cleared of debris at frequent intervals and that the pump is switched off when it starts sucking air. Remove the remaining sludge (a plastic dustpan is very handy for this) and search it for inconspicuous tench, newts or other creatures you may want to preserve.

Whatever other reason there may have been for emptying the pond – repairing a leak perhaps – refilling should commence as soon as practicable after that job has been completed. While filling is going on the plants can be tidied up. Deal with baskets of oxygenators first since they are at most risk of shrivelling, and get them back into water; then lilies and other surfacing plants, then marginals. Cut off shoots and roots straying from containers. Assuming this action takes place during the growing season, tip out, split up and replant in new soil any plants that are overgrown or starved. As they are dealt with return the containers to the refilled pond: they are not needed in the temporary one. If a dechlorinator such as Haloex can be added to the refilled pond, fish can be returned to it 24 hours later since it should by then be at the same temperature as the temporary pond. Without a dechlorinator, wait three days before returning the fish.

Vital Statistics
The important facts about a pond are its surface area and its volume in gallons. The surface area indicates the number of plants it will require and the maximum number of fish it should be expected to support. Dosage with algicides or any other chemical treatment is based on gallonage and, while there is always some safety margin, it is necessary to know with reasonable accuracy how many gallons a pond holds if chemical treatment is not to be either too weak to do any good or too strong to be safe. It is not difficult to work out the vital statistics of ponds of regular geometrical shapes; the more irregular and complicated the shape the more it becomes a matter of guesswork rather than calculation.

Surface area
The surface area of a rectangular pond is the length multiplied by the width. For example: a rectangular pond 8 feet long and 5 feet wide has a surface area of 40 square feet.

The surface area of a triangular pond is half of the length of any side multiplied by the shortest distance between that side and the opposite corner.

The surface area of a circular pond is half of the diameter (the distance across the middle) multiplied by itself and then multiplied by 3.142.

For a circular pond measuring 12 feet across, therefore, the area is $6 \times 6 \times 3.142 = 113$ square feet. For all practical purposes it is enough to multiply by 3 instead of 3.142. In this case it would give 108 square feet instead of 113.

The surface area of an oval pond is arrived at by adding the length to the width and dividing by two, and then treating the answer as if it was the diameter of a circular pond. Thus, for an oval pond 12 feet long and 8 feet wide over-all: $12 + 8 = 20 \div 2 = 10$. Calculate as for a circle 10 feet in diameter: $5 \times 5 \times 3.142 = 78.55$ square feet (or $5 \times 5 \times 3 = 75$ square feet, which is close enough).

Sometimes complicated shapes can be broken down into several simple shapes. An L-shaped pond can be treated as two rectangles. One shaped like a dumb-bell can be calculated easily enough as a rectangle and two circles.

Volume (gallonage)

The volume, or gallonage, of the pond is calculated by multiplying the surface area by the average water depth (measured in the same units of course) and multiplying the answer by $6\frac{1}{4}$ (for Imperial gallons) or by $7\frac{1}{2}$ for U.S. gallons. The average water depth may be difficult to estimate precisely. If half the pond was 2 feet deep and half 1 foot deep, the average of $1\frac{1}{2}$ would be easy enough to arrive at. However, if most of it was 2 feet deep and only a small part 1 foot deep, the average would not be $1\frac{1}{2}$ but something very close to 2 feet; so close that you might as well use 2 for the purposes of calculation and then knock about a twentieth off the answer, to be on the safe side. Take, for example, a circular pond 8 feet in diameter, water depth 2 feet except for a shelf on one side 9 inches deep.

Surface area is $4 \times 4 \times 3.142 = 50.27$ square feet.

Volume is $50.27 \times 2 \times 6.25 = 628$, but knock off about a twentieth to allow for the shelves, and the answer is 600 gallons Imperial $= 720$ gallons U.S.

It is worth going to a little trouble to calculate the surface area and gallonage of your pond with care and then record the answers where you will be able to find them when you want them again.

8

A Water Gardener's Year

Winter

As winter cold grips the pond, fish become less and less active. Their need for both food and oxygen falls with the temperature. They can perfectly well survive the cold, resting virtually in a state of torpor, and living off their fat, until higher temperatures restore activity and natural food sources. They will be at risk, however, if the pond freezes over. A skin of ice that disappears by midday presents no problem; it is the sheet of ice that persists for weeks (or even days) that causes trouble, because it prevents the normal exchange of gases at the surface. Oxygen cannot get in and gases in the water cannot escape. If the pond contains a lot of decaying material the by-products of bacterial action may include methane and hydrogen sulphide which, unable to escape into the atmosphere, suffocate the fish. Such tragedies can be prevented by keeping a hole open in the ice. Hitting the ice is not the way to do this; every year fish are killed by shock waves from the thoughtless pounding of ice with hammers. And every year pond liners are punctured by garden forks plunged carelessly through ice that was not as thick as it seemed.

A better method is to stand a metal container on the ice (a cocoa tin is ideal) and fill it with boiling water. It will go through several inches of ice in minutes. There are two ways to use the hole thus achieved. One is to siphon out water to lower the pond level a few inches below the ice. In theory you then get a greenhouse effect that prevents the new water surface from freezing over. It may work if the ice is strong enough; or the ice collapses and the pond freezes again with less water depth below the ice than there was originally. The second and highly recommended way to utilise the hole is to insert into it a pond heater. This, a small immersion heater of 125 or 150 watts suspended under a float, will enlarge the hole and keep it open, however cold it gets and whether you are in attendance or not. (A heater requires mains voltage electricity.)

A thick sheet of ice can pose a threat to the pond structure, if it is made of concrete, and particularly if the sides are vertical. Expanding ice will crack inflexible concrete as easily as it bursts water pipes. A

161

pond heater will help to avoid this. Alternatively damage can be avoided by floating on the water compressible objects which will absorb the pressure and take the strain off the walls. To be effective they must cover a reasonable area. Planks and logs are ideal, as are large polystyrene boxes, provided they are ballasted with pebbles to prevent them riding on top of the water. A floating tennis ball or a ballasted detergent bottle is no help except to leave, on being pulled out of the ice, a neat hole in which to insert a heater. The bottle may need to have its top removed and hot water poured in before it will come free.

If there is no power supply for a heater the best tactic is to cover an end or corner of the pond with polythene or, where severe weather is likely, with planks and such insulating material as straw, polystyrene sheet, or even a thick layer of newspapers. If the pond is small enough to make complete covering practicable it should be of transparent polythene to allow some light in.

Spring

As the water temperature creeps up fish begin to stir and forage half-heartedly for food. They have used up their reserves: their resistance to disease is at its lowest ebb and at this stage they can be vulnerable to fungus. The temperature can rise sufficiently to start fish moving about and using up energy without getting high enough to get them feeding well. There is little the pond-owner can do if signs of fungus are seen. If the spring cannot make up its mind, the use of the pond heater or a polythene tent may lift the water temperature of a small pond enough to stimulate fish appetites. The owner must be ready to respond to any sign that fish are looking for food. It must be offered sparingly until it is obvious that they are hungry; then they can be given as much as they are prepared to take of live *Daphnia*, chopped earthworm and flake food. Pellets of the Japanese formulation for Koi carp are excellent for all pondfish and much more satisfactory than trout pellets. Generous feeding and a varied diet quickly restore resistance to disease and bring fish into breeding condition.

Ponds that have held a lot of decaying vegetation during the winter may have inky black water, or it may have a milky appearance. It is most likely in small ponds with masses of unchecked plant growth; large ponds usually have less in relation to the water volume. Water overburdened with the by-products of decay can be a danger to fish, and a half water change is recommended. There are, in fact, few ponds which would not benefit from this spring treatment (see pp. 143–4).

Summary

Summer

The early summer is the ideal time both for planting new stock and for tidying, dividing and replanting the old; for adding fertilising pellets to rejuvenate tired lilies (see p. 146); and to tackle, when it eventually becomes necessary, the complete clear-out as described on pp. 157–9. But more than anything else the summer is the time to look, to observe, to enjoy the pond. Vigilance is essential if such nuisances as *Dytiscus* beetles and larvae are to be spotted and dealt with. Only close and prolonged observation will make it possible for the eyes suddenly to bring into focus the tiny half-coloured glass splinters that are fish fry lurking among plant stems. Absolute quiet and stillness are essential for the successful observation of aquatic creatures, and this can best be achieved in a reclining position.

Some observations may need to be followed by action. The sight of driving or spawning fish should instigate the removal of either the parent fish or the spawn to the reserve pond; or at least a mental note to *make* a reserve pond. Seeing lily leaves furrowed by water lily beetles and skeletonised by midge larvae should stimulate action as described on pp. 144 and 145, or the pondering of possible alternatives. Is there handy a piece of metal mesh heavy enough to sink the foliage for a few days and open enough to permit fish to pick off the insects? A bowl-shaped wire frame intended for training weeping roses works very well on the smaller lilies. Or dare one risk a whiff of insecticide? I did, using pyrethrum, with the help of a sheet of polystyrene with a large hole in the centre. Dropped over the lily the hole exposed the affected leaves, with very little water showing. A whiff from the spray at close range misted the leaves and the border of polystyrene caught what might have tainted the water. There were no ill-effects, except to the beetles and larvae.

The sudden development of masses of blanketweed, even in ponds which have been going for years without it, is one of the mysteries of water gardening. However, there can be few gardening jobs more interesting than its removal. The first step is to push a stout stick into the stuff. A broom handle (which might be thought too smooth for the job) is ideal. Rotate it and it winds the silkweed round it in a steadily thickening wad, drawing the green strands from far and wide. When you lift it out (which requires all the strength of the broom handle) you can either dump it straight on the compost heap or put it in a wheelbarrow for sorting out. (The latter will involve you in the difficult question of what to keep and what to cast out).

Autumn

With the tide of plant growth on the ebb care must be taken to keep the amount of dead foliage in the pond to a minimum. The practical value of oxygenators is over: cut them back hard and throw out what would otherwise decompose in the water. Late August is not too soon for this: do it by mid-September at the latest. If it is practicable remove the spent blooms and leaves of water lilies as they die off. When marginals are browned by frost cut them down to water level.

Fish should be plump and sleek but there is less natural food now. As long as the water stays warm and they have hearty appetites give them all the food they want to build up their reserves for the winter. And give them the tonic of a half water change. Through the summer months they have been feeding and excreting and urinating. Their waste products have been broken down by bacteria into carbon dioxide, water, ammonia, and ammonium compounds. Other bacteria have then oxidised the ammonia to nitrites. Most of the nitrites, which are poisonous, have been converted by yet other types of bacteria into nitrates, which are harmless to fish as well as being essential food for plants. Some nitrites, however, remain unconverted and cause a degree of pollution. How serious a degree depends on the number and size of the fish in relation to the water volume. There may be very little danger but everything possible should be done to reduce the problems fish have to face if the pond freezes over. Changing half to two-thirds of the water in the autumn is highly desirable in ponds which are heavily stocked with fish.

One other touch the fish will appreciate is the provision of some shelter, if the pond bottom is devoid of rockwork. A few clay pipes about 4 inches in diameter scattered on the bottom make excellent refuges for torpid fish—and boltholes from the threat of herons or other predators.

It remains to remove the pump, clean it and store it for the winter; to connect up the pond heater, though it will only be switched on when the weather is extreme; and to net over the pond with small-mesh plastic netting to keep out falling leaves. It can be removed when the trees are bare except in areas where winter protection is needed against the activities of gulls and herons.

Metric Conversion Table

1 inch = 2.54 cm
1 foot = 30.5 cm
1 square foot = 0.093 m²
1 square yard = 9 square feet — 0.84 m²
1 quart = 1.14 litres
1 Imperial gallon = 1.2 U.S. gallons = 4.54 litres
1 bushel = 32 quarts = 1.28 cu. ft. = 36.4 litres
1 lb = 0.45 kg
1 cwt = 50.8 kg

Index

Figures in bold refer to colour plates; hwl = hardy water lily; dbt = day-blooming tropical; nbt = night-blooming tropical.